English in fact
Exam Practice Papers

Steve Merrell with Doug Bloom

Tried and tested practice papers to refine examination skills and aid assessment.

Publication Information

Copyright Note
Reproduction from this resource is allowed for use within individual purchasing institutions only. Copyright is strictly reserved for all other purposes, and permission must be obtained from the publishers for any other use.

Published by Carel Press Ltd
4 Hewson St,
Carlisle CA2 5AU
Tel 01228 538928

Carel_Press@compuserve.com

© 1998 Steve Merrell & Doug Bloom

Cover and design: Fiona Wilson Design
Illustrations: Craig Mitchell
Printed by MFP Ltd, Manchester
Printing number: 1 2 3 4 5 6 7 8 9 10

Environmental Information

This book is printed on 100% recycled paper which is made entirely from printed waste, & is not re-bleached. Using recycled paper saves trees, water & energy while reducing air pollution & landfill.

British Library Cataloguing in Publication Data
Merrell, Steve
English in Fact: practice papers for GCSE/Standard Grade examinations
1. English Language - examinations, questions etc.
1. Title II Bloom, Doug
428'.0076

ISBN 1-872365-47-7

CAREL PRESS

English in fact — Exam Practice Papers

Contents

Introduction	3

Foundation Level

One for the record	5
Questions	7
Answers	8
Peace of mind while you're away	10
Questions	12
Answers	13
Used cars	15
Questions	17
Answers	18
The cost of a drink	20
Questions	23
Answers	24
I want my son put in prison!	26
Questions	28
Answers	29
117 days adrift	31
Questions	33
Answers	34

Higher Level

What's in a name?	36
Questions	38
Answers	39
All the rage	41
Questions	43
Answers	44
The national lottery	46
Questions	49
Answers	50
Sharing not buying	51
Questions	54
Answers	55
A journey along the Silk Route	57
Questions	59
Answers	60
Happy Christmas?	62
Questions	63
Answers	64

Dual Level

Winning smiles	66
When money's the root of all evil...	67
Foundation Level Questions	68
Foundation Level Answers	69
Higher Level Questions	71
Higher Level Answers	72
Walk to school	74
Foundation Level Questions	79
Foundation Level Answers	80
Higher Level Questions	81
Higher Level Answers	82
Woman with a winning punch	84
Foundation Level Questions	85
Foundation Level Answers	86
Higher Level Questions	89
Higher Level Answers	90
Can Teletubbies really be good for young children?	91
Foundation Level Questions	94
Foundation Level Answers	95
Higher Level Questions	98
Higher Level Answers	99
Sample essay 1	100
Sample essay 2	101
Commentary on sample essays 1 & 2	102
Sample essay 3	103
Commentary on sample essay 3	104

English in fact — Exam Practice Papers

The aim of this book is to sharpen students' skills in approaching examination papers for GCSE/Standard Grade English Language examinations. In particular in approaching that part of the examination which is based on factual material, hence the title *English in Fact*.

The format is flexible enough to be adapted to a variety of examination requirements but should also provide a familiar structured pattern to help build the student's ability in answering examination questions.

Many teachers will find it valuable to have this substantial resource of factual material, taken from genuine and current sources and providing variety in tone, style and content. The reading material and questions have been selected to provide stimulus across the ability range. In some cases, it would have been tempting to edit the sources to improve punctuation or grammar, however, in the interests of authenticity, these have been left unless they would actually have been misleading.

The book contains six Foundation and six Higher level papers, with four 'crossover' papers which include questions at both levels. These last may be especially useful in deciding the appropriate examination entry level for students, particularly those close to the borderline.

In general, the Foundation tier (Grades C - G) have easier reading material, with a more limited range of vocabulary. The length of a piece is not, however, indicative of its complexity. The Higher tier (Grades D – A*) have more complex extracts and more demanding questions to complete in the set time.

Times have been left blank on the question papers to allow the most flexible use. It may well be that teachers will wish to adjust the time given according to the ability of the group, the stage they are at in their course or merely the time available in a lesson. This is also a useful means of differentiation within the group. A time is, however, offered on the answer sheet, based on the experience of using these papers within schools. In most cases the examination papers can be completed in under 90 minutes - around a double period in many schools.

Each examination paper is accompanied by an advisory mark scheme and a guide to how the numbers can relate to grades. These cannot be definitive. Pupils can always surprise us with their interpretations and mark schemes cannot take account of every variation.

Although these papers have been given trial runs with students and amended in the light of their answers, should a student provide an original and suitable interpretation then marks should be awarded. For the longer answers, where a choice is provided, we advise teachers to read all of the mark scheme keeping in mind the top grading to see whether the student achieves the potential of the answer or falls short in some areas.

Despite the limitations of mark schemes in English, they do offer substantial benefits:

- they save teacher time, making marking quicker and easier
- they promote consistency of marking within sets of papers, across groups and even across years
- because they aid consistency they are also helpful in standardisation of marking across a department, especially important for formal assessment
- they can be used as a teaching aid to show pupils what is required in order to achieve certain grades (see below)

The mark scheme can be duplicated for student use - it is often useful for them to see how a paper is marked. If they themselves are involved in marking, they begin to build up a mark scheme in their heads and to apply it to their own work. Being involved in the marking process also allows them to understand more clearly the relationship between the number of marks available and the number of points that should be made, as well as helping them to interpret the demands to explain, justify or give examples.

In addition, there are three sample student essays with commentary for class discussion. These have proved to be very valuable for students to mark themselves and to use as models in considering how to answer. We hope that students will identify the weaknesses as well as the strengths and apply this analysis to their own work.

Regular practice with test papers can build a student's confidence in answering test questions and improve skills in working to a set time and focusing on the key points required. This book will benefit both teachers and students in this respect, as well as offering material which is relevant and intrinsically interesting.

Steve Merrell
Doug Bloom

Notes on using some of the resources

Peace of mind — Page 10
This is one of the easiest reading resources and may be a good starting point for students unfamiliar with this question paper approach. Teachers may find it a suitable bridge between the Key Stage 3 SATs paper and GCSE/Standard Grade.

The cost of a drink — Page 20
This is taken from two booklets, distributed by the police. The first section is from a booklet aimed at older teenagers and the second section (Alcohol and Drugs) is from a booklet for parents. In trials we found this paper the longest one to read and 'digest' for Foundation students.

National lottery — Page 46
This is a demanding article for students and so one task was set for the extended writing although a choice is included within it. As a matter of interest, the matter of unequal funding to the north and the south of the country was raised again in Parliament on April 7th, 1998 although no action was suggested.

Sharing not buying — Page 51
There is a lot to read in this article so the first section only contains three questions. This is a good paper for showing students the importance of noting the value of marks for each question and, when asked, to refer closely to the resource material.

Happy Christmas? — Page 62
The source for this article and the content is explained on the question paper. Teachers might want to define a few of the words in the piece for the students (such as *coup de grace*) although most of the other difficult words can be defined by their context. It may be helpful to explain the nature of Radio Four and its likely listener profile.

Walk to school — Page 74
The aim of this paper is to allow the teacher to focus on the different demands of explicit and implicit questions. There are more of both kinds of question in this section, and, as a result, there is no room for the normal "extension question". It is likely that the ability to cope with implicit questions is one of the main signs of suitability for the Higher tier, so this section may be of particular interest for mixed ability and middle band classes to determine which level best suits each student.
This section uses three passages taken from a larger pack on walking to school:

	NUMBER AND TYPE OF QUESTIONS
Air pollution monitoring results more	five explicit factual and two complex questions
Walk Talk 1	three questions involving reordering and collating information
Walking to school; the parent's tale:	five questions requiring skills of implicit understanding.

It is suggested that the first two passages comprise the Foundation tier paper, with the third passage added for the Higher tier. The performance of "borderline" students on the third passage will thus be particularly significant. This point is illustrated in the guide to grade boundaries at the end of the mark schemes.

Woman with a winning punch — Page 84
Both Foundation and Higher tier questions have been set on this passage. This provides an opportunity to set the same passage for a whole group, which may prove useful for discussion (and even assessed speaking and listening tasks). It may also be helpful in placing borderline candidates in the appropriate tier. On Monday 30 March 1998, Jane Couch won her case for sexual discrimination against the professional boxing authorities. An industrial tribunal ruled that applications for licenses from women should be treated on the same basis as those from men. Jane Couch can claim a points victory for Round 1 but there is to be an appeal.

There is an example student essay for the extended question on page 103.

Teletubbies — Page 91
The comments above on *Woman with a winning punch* also apply to this paper but Higher level students have an additional section to read and answer questions on. The extended tasks are the same and a note about the marking is added.

Two example student essays with a detailed commentary have been added and highlight some of the more frequent errors made when answering this paper (pages 100-102).

Sample essays
We have found it useful to put the students in the role of teacher and to give them examples of work to appraise.
Our instructions were:
Read through this essay and add your comments in the margins. Tick any good points. If you spot a mistake, circle it. If a point has not been made well underline it and explain why. If you think a point is in the wrong place, put an arrow to show where it should go. Give the essay a mark out of 20 (Essays 1 and 3) or 30 (Essay 2).

Sample essay 1 & 2
These answers are based on an actual essays submitted for a mock examination. We have included many of the technical errors that appear in essays of this standard. The technical errors have not been noted as they are (we hope) obvious.

In our trials, we gave students Sample Essay 1 to consider first. Although they often picked up the technical errors they still awarded it considerably more marks than it was worth. They revised their opinions considerably after reading the second essay.

Sample Essay 3
This essay by Year 11 student, Barry Gibbons, was completed within one hour with the rest of the question paper for the Higher tier. Barry's original approach and authentic news story style should strike the reader as being work of a very high quality – Grade A. To be more specific we have taken the marking criteria for this question and given examples from Barry's essay. This may be an interesting exercise to try with a class to get them to see the elements needed for a top essay, rather than just an overall view of the piece.

Additional factual material suitable for use in the teaching of English can be found in the Essential Articles series from Carel Press.

One for the record

Kriss Akabusi spends more of his time these days presenting records on TV than breaking them on the athletics track. But he still knows what it takes...

If there's one thing I've learned from presenting the latest series of Record Breakers, it's that people will go to almost any lengths to get their name in the record books. And it's not always just because they're determined to be the best.

I first got on to the programme as a result of the British men's 4 x 400m relay record in Tokyo in 1991. We were invited to appear on Record Breakers and we really enjoyed ourselves. When I retired from athletics the following year, the producer rang up and asked me if I'd like to co-present it with Cheryl Baker. I jumped at the chance, because I'd always loved Record Breakers ever since I first watched Roy Castle as a kid.

If you wanna be the best...

Back then, just like any other kid, I wanted to be a record breaker. I had no real idea I'd one day hold the British 400m hurdles record. Nobody's beaten it yet, but they will... when you're an old man, the youngsters eventually come along and surpass you! It's something I'm very proud of – it helps me understand why people go to any lengths to set their own records.

You hear about a record you can beat, and as you get closer and closer to achieving it, you can get a bit obsessed. Record-chasers are always very dedicated and highly focused people, and I admire them for it. In most things I do, I'm the same – if I don't have a goal, my attention wanders very quickly.

Presenting the show means a lot of world travel showcasing record attempts, all

One for the record

of which have to be properly witnessed and authenticated. You see some pretty weird ones: I remember Roy Castle telling me about a cowpat throwing contest he'd attended in Canada. This would be odd enough, but he said it got really weird when it started to rain and the contestants were trying to dry off their prized cowpats with a convection heater. The trouble was, only the edges would dry, and the centres kept falling out and covering the throwers in dung...

The strangest ones I've seen are men trying to throw beer mats a record distance, and a bloke in New York's Central Park breaking the world record for forward rolls. He managed to do forward rolls over a whole mile in under 20 minutes. I've also witnessed a 'memory man' who can memorise the exact order of every card in every suit in up to ten packs of cards. That was pretty astonishing.

Less amusing – for me, at least! – was a custard pie throwing record attempt in Covent Garden. I was one of the unlucky victims who got wheeled out every now and then to get pies chucked at them, and it lasted a whole hour. OK, so that wasn't exactly as glamourous as the 100m sprint, but to break any record you need the motivation to go on when things aren't going well.

Practice makes perfect, and you have to work hard, staying very focused on the task. Breaking a record isn't easy, so it's best to choose an activity you enjoy, and keep the target in mind. But most of all, to use Roy's famous words, 'Dedication's what you need'.

If you wanna beat the rest...

Of course, at the last Olympic Games, people were saying that was Britain's problem: we aren't dedicated enough to win events or set records any more. I do think that's unfair, because as with all sports there are passing phases. Stars like Linford Christie and Colin Jackson may be coming to the end of their careers at the top, but we've got new up-and-coming athletes. We saw a few youngsters making fireworks for the first time, and I think in four years we'll be up there again. There'll certainly be more records for Britain in future.

Having said that, some of the records I admire most aren't ones you see in the books. The first men on the moon, for instance, were breaking ground by establishing a record nobody had even imagined possible a few years before.

Unlike athletics, where you're essentially trying your hardest to improve on something that others have done before you, going into space is what I'd call a 'proper first'. It's all very well sending animals, or even robots, but can you imagine the first guys who jumped up and flew out into space, risking their lives..?

Even when I was in competitive athletics full time, you would never have caught me doing anything that adventurous or daring. My feet are firmly on the ground!

Focus

One for the record

Time: _____

Read 'One for the Record'. Answer questions 1 - 4, then choose a, b or c from question 5.

1. Select four record breaking events that Kriss has witnessed.
   (4 marks)

2. Select a record breaking contest, mentioned in the article, that Kriss hasn't seen.
   (1 mark)

3. Select three qualities Kriss says you need to be a record breaker.
   (3 marks)

4. Write two or three paragraphs explaining how this article is made interesting for the reader. (You can earn more marks if you support your ideas with examples.)
   (7 marks)

Answer one question below.

5a. You are the organiser for a Weird Record-Breaking Day in your local area. You can invent all the special events, such as Welly Boot Throwing. Write an article for the local paper that explains all about the day which is coming up and why it will be worth attending.
   (20 marks)

   or

5b. You are the coach for a local league Under 13 football or netball side. Write the talk that you would give to the team before they are about to undertake a major match. Some of Kriss's ideas might help you.
   (20 marks)

   or

5c. Are cow pat throwing and forward rolls proper records? Consider these and other records and discuss whether people are being silly or sensible in trying to set or break records. You can write the piece as a discussion between two people with opposite views.
   (20 marks)

One for the record — Foundation Level – Answers

One for the record Marking Suggestions

Advised Time: 60 minutes

1. Select four record breaking events that Kriss has witnessed: *(4 marks)*
   - beer mat throwing
   - forward rolls
   - memory man
   - custard pie throwing

   Note: You may allow his own 400m hurdles record but not as an addition to the 4.

2. Select a record breaking contest, mentioned in the article, that Kriss hasn't seen. *(1 mark)*
   - cow pat throwing.

3. Select three qualities Kriss says you need to be a record breaker: *(3 marks - any three below which do not have to be given as quotations.)*
   - very dedicated
   - need the motivation
   - highly focused
   - practice makes perfect
   - go to almost any length
   - determined to be the best.

4. Write two or three paragraphs explaining how this article is made interesting for the reader. *(You can earn more marks if you support your ideas with examples.)* *(7 marks available - a feature supported by an example is worth 2 marks.)*
   - *chatty, spoken style, informal language e.g. I watched Roy Castle as a kid*
   - *variety of topics - the programme, his own achievement, the weird, the comic, his views*
   - *humorous events*
   - *backs up points with examples, repeats a point*
   - *brief article, subject matter is clear*
   - *sub-headline, 'But he still knows what it takes ...' raises curiosity*
   - *visually interesting - the illustration.*

5a. You are the organiser for a Weird Record-Breaking Day in your local area. You can invent all the special events, such as Welly Boot Throwing. Write an article for the local paper that explains all about the day which is coming up and why it will be worth attending.

   20 - 16 *Answers will contain a majority of these points:*
   - *suitable newspaper style layout, e.g. headline and possibly sub-headline*
   - *engaging opening paragraph to news story*
   - *content is interesting, inventive (even if they have borrowed events from the article) and is written with a style that would make the reader curious*
   - *the article may make some references to the Record Breakers programme (use of the article)*
   - *mention of time, date and place and possibly entrance prices or contact number*
   - *varied and interesting expression. They may include comments from some of the participants*
   - *spelling good and careful use of punctuation*
   - *very few errors.*

   15 -11 *Answers will contain a majority of these points:*
   - *some attempt at a newspaper style layout*
   - *work may show qualities of the highest band but there is less development, e.g. events are listed but not made to sound enticing*
   - *it should still read like a news article although it hasn't the concision of an edited article*
   - *arrangements have been added, date, time, place etc.*
   - *technically fair at the top end of this band. The article should be paragraphed. There may be weaknesses in punctuation and spelling of some common words.*

   10 - 6 *Answers will contain a majority of these points:*
   - *an awareness that the style is meant to be a newspaper article but too much time may have been wasted on drawing a photograph or elaborate headline*
   - *the piece is too short or superficial*
   - *article does not have the correct tone for a newspaper e.g. written in the first person*
   - *technically weak in places with errors in punctuation and some simple words (for the lower end of this band)*
   - *low marks if the article reports that the event has taken place.*

   5 or less.
   - *unlikely to read like a news article*
   - *little planning and few ideas*
   - *technical errors hamper the understanding.*

5b. You are the coach for a local league Under 13 football or netball side. Write the talk that you would give to the team before they are about to undertake a major match. Some of Kriss's ideas might help you.

   20 - 16 *Answers will contain a majority of these points:*
   - *good, stirring and encouraging tone, a mixture of friendliness, advice and instruction*
   - *they could quote Kriss's advice from the last column e.g. you need the motivation to go on when things aren't going well. Dedication's what you need*
   - *varied expression. Particularly reward attempts at speech technique such as repetition for effect*
   - *awareness of the age and expectations of the team through the language used*
   - *inventive, mentioning strategies and previous training ideas*
   - *spelling good and careful use of punctuation. Very few errors.*

Foundation Level – Answers
One for the record

15 - 11 Answers will contain a majority of these points:
- the right tone and general approach although it will lack the subtlety to be in the top band
- some advice may be repetitive in ideas or expression
- less well planned not giving the best advice near the end of the talk
- less awareness of the age of the audience
- technically fair at the top end of this band. The piece should be paragraphed.

10 - 6 Answers will contain a majority of these points:
- the tone is unsuitable. It does not sound like a team talk, more like a small essay
- work is short or repetitive
- unlikely to have used anything from the article
- points are badly organised or contradictory
- technically weak in places with errors in punctuation and some simple words (for the lower end of this band).

5 - or less
- a misunderstanding of the task
- very brief work / Little planning and few ideas
- technical errors hamper the understanding.

5c. Are cow pat throwing and forward rolls proper records? Consider these and other records and discuss whether people are being silly or sensible in trying to set or break records. You can write the piece as a discussion between two people with opposite views.

20 - 16 Answers will contain a majority of these points:
- argument has been planned
- a good attempt at seeing both sides of the argument
- good use made of the article, such as to justify points
- imaginative or knowledgeable in discussing other records beyond the two in the question
- argument has a conclusion (good time management)
- spelling good and careful use of punctuation. Very few errors.

15 - 11 Answers will contain a majority of these points:
- a number of good ideas and opinions but not in the best order
- views may not be justified
- discussion or essay may peter out after stating a view early on and the work becomes repetitive
- technically fair at the top end of this band. The piece should be paragraphed.

10 - 6 Answers will contain a majority of these points:
- overall view is expressed early on with little justification or a muddled or contradictory view
- there is unlikely to be reference to the article
- keeps to the two records in the question and no others
- technically weak in places with errors in punctuation and some simple words (for the lower end of this band).

5 - or below
- few comments, poorly structured or incomplete
- technical errors hamper the understanding.

Guide to grade boundaries	
35 - 30	C
29 - 24	D
23 - 18	E
17 - 12	F
11 - 8	G
Below 8	U

Peace of Mind While You're Away

PEACE OF MIND WHILE YOU'RE AWAY
Advice on keeping your home secure

Everyone needs a holiday some time. And however much you like your home, there's nothing like a change of surroundings.

But you want to come home and find everything as you left it. Four out of five burglaries occur when a house or flat is empty, so don't advertise that you're away on holiday.

PLAN AHEAD

The checklist opposite will help you to keep your home secure. Read it now so that you can plan ahead. Then tick off the items just before you go.

HELP FROM YOUR NEIGHBOURS

It's also a good idea to get help from your neighbours. All you have to do is fill in the card on the next page and give it to a friend or neighbour. It asks them to keep an eye on your home while you're away.

You could also ask them to collect post left in the letter-box, sweep up leaves, even mow the lawn and generally make the place look lived in.

You can repay the favour by doing the same for them. Warn your key-holding neighbour not to put your surname, address or even your house number on your keys in case they fall into the wrong hands.

Is there a neighbourhood watch scheme where you live? It could help you keep your home secure while you're away, and has many other crime prevention and community benefits.

Tell your local police station that you'll be away.

CHECKLIST

1 Help reduce the risk of your home being broken into by taking some simple home security measures. The free handbook *Practical Ways to Crack Crime* has over a hundred tips on preventing crime. To get a copy, ask your local police station or write to the Home Office, Crack Crime, PO Box 999, Sudbury, Suffolk, CO10 6FS, or ring 0181-569 7000.

2 Leave small valuable items, like jewellery, on deposit at the bank, or consider installing a small floor safe. Don't lock internal doors or desks – they may be forced if someone does break in.

3 Mark any other valuable items with your postcode followed by the house number or the first two letters of the house name. Then if they are stolen and later found, the police can identify and return them to you. Use the right security marker – DIY shops sell property marking kits. Ask your local crime prevention officer for 'postcoded property' warning stickers to display in the front and back windows of your house. Also take photos of all valuable items. This is particularly important for those which may be unsuitable for marking.

4 Arrange for pets to be properly looked after.

5 Cut the lawns before you go.

6 Cancel deliveries of milk, newspapers, etc., discreetly – don't announce your departure to a shop full of people. Only tell people who need to know you're going away.

Checklist continued overleaf >

Peace of Mind While You're Away

CHECKLIST (continued)

7 Make sure your house looks occupied. Closed curtains in the daytime make it look as if no one is home. It is worthwhile to get automatic time switches to switch lights - and a radio - on and off in downstairs rooms.

8 Don't leave valuable items like TVs, videos or hi-fi visible through windows.

9 Lock the garage and shed with proper security locks, after putting all your tools safely away so that they cannot be used to break into your house. If you <u>have</u> to leave a ladder out, put it on its side and lock it to a secure fixture with a 'close-shackle' padlock and heavy-duty chain.

10 Don't have your home address showing on your luggage for the outward journey. Put this only on the inside of your cases.

11 Finally, lock all outside doors and windows. If you have a burglar alarm, make sure that it is set – and that you have told the police who the keyholder is.

And just before you actually set off, it's worth allowing a quiet couple of minutes on the doorstep to check you've done all you had to do and taken everything you need with you.

For a free copy of the 40-page Handbook, "Practical Ways to Crack Crime", ask your local police station or write to the Home Office, Crack Crime, PO Box 999, Sudbury, Suffolk, CO10 6FS or ring 0181-569 7000

Dear neighbour

GOOD NEIGHBOUR CARD

Signed _____

Home Address _____

Thank you for your help - I'll look after your home when **you're** away.

I will be away from _____

Returning on _____

Holiday address(es), dates and telephone numbers
_____
_____
_____

Holiday company telephone _____

Car make, colour and registration _____

Other information _____
_____

Please keep this card in a safe place - thank you. (If you have my spare key, please <u>don't</u> mark it with my surname, house number or anything similar.)

English in Fact © Carel Press   11

Peace of Mind

Foundation Level – Questions

Time: _____

Read all of 'Peace Of Mind While You're Away'. Answer questions 1, 2 and 3. Choose a or b from question 4.

1. List five ways neighbours can help keep your home secure while you are away.
   (5 marks)

2. Find and list ten ways to increase your security which may not cost anything.
   (10 marks)

3. Choose two of the items from the Checklist that you think offer the best advice. Explain carefully why you think these two are best in comparison to the others.
   (9 marks)

Answer one question below.

4a. You have been asked to help set up a Neighbourhood Watch scheme.
   Write a friendly but useful letter to the local people about a meeting you intend to hold and what they might do to help the scheme work well.
   (20 marks)

   or

4b. Could schools improve on security for students' and teachers' property? What are the weaknesses in your school and how could they be solved? Write this as an article for the school magazine.
   (20 marks)

Peace of Mind While You're Away Marking Suggestions   Advised Time: 60 minutes

1. List five ways neighbours can help keep your home secure while you are away.
   (5 marks - any five of the eight below)
   - make sure they have the Dear Neighbour card
   - keep an eye on your place
   - push through post and newspapers left in the letter box
   - collect milk and deliveries left on the step
   - call the police if they are suspicious
   - sweep up leaves
   - mow the lawn
   - make the place look lived in.

2. Find and list ten ways to increase your security which may not cost anything.
   (ten marks, one for each point up to ten marks)
   - not put your name and address on keys
   - inform Neighbourhood Watch
   - inform the police
   - send off / collect / phone for the free handbook
   - mark personal possessions with your postcode and house number
   - put luggage labels on the inside of your case
   - cancel deliveries of milk
   - don't announce publicly that you will be away / don't advertise that your home is unoccupied
   - keep your curtains open
   - lock all outside doors and windows
   - don't leave valuable items visible
   - lock sheds and garages
   - make sure tools are safely stored away
   - secure ladders
   - cut the lawns before you go.

3. Choose two of the items from the Checklist that you think offer the best advice. Explain carefully why you think these two are best in comparison to the others. (9 marks)

9 - 7 marks
   - two points chosen and both explained well.
   - some consideration of why these two pieces of advice are more worthwhile than the others.

6 - 4 marks
   - two points chosen but possibly one explained more fully than the other.
   - little explanation of why these two points are better than the others.

3 - 1 marks
   - fewer than two points chosen.
   - very little explanation, if any, of why they are better than the others.

Note: There is a strong argument that sending for the booklet is one of the best pieces of advice as it is free and contains over 100 pieces of advice.

4a. You have been asked to set up a Neighbourhood Watch scheme. Write a friendly but useful letter to the local people about a meeting you intend to hold and what they might do to help the scheme work well.

20 - 16 marks Answers will contain a majority of these points:
   - correct letter layout
   - audience clearly targeted
   - understanding of what a Neighbourhood Watch scheme does
   - tone is friendly such as a welcoming first paragraph
   - details of meeting, date etc.
   - ideas and examples to promote thinking for the meeting
   - at the top end of this band, work is technically very good with few errors in punctuation and spelling, at the bottom end there are a few errors in common words.

15 - 11 marks Answers will contain a majority of these points:
   - correct letter layout, at worst it begins with a 'Dear ...', even if there is no address
   - letter is likely to be more functional and direct
   - ideas / events may not be assembled in a sensible order
   - most details of meeting included
   - for lowest marks, there must be at least two ideas to help the Neighbourhood Watch scheme
   - work is technically fair but common and repeated errors in the lower part of this band, particularly in punctuation.

10 - 6 marks Answers will contain a majority of these points:
   - some sense of it being a letter
   - probably very short and perfunctory
   - maybe some of the meeting details are missing, e.g. date, place
   - at least one idea to help the Neighbourhood Watch scheme such as encouragement to the readers to attend the meeting
   - technically weak although the mistakes do not hamper the overall meaning.

Peace of Mind — Foundation Level – Answers

5 - or below
- *a misunderstanding of the task or low quality, unplanned work.*

5 - or below
- *a misunderstanding of the task or low quality, unplanned work.*

4b. Could schools improve on security for students' and teachers' property? What are the weaknesses in your school and how could they be solved? Write this as an article for the school magazine.

Guide to grade boundaries	
44 – 39	C
38 – 33	D
32 – 27	E
26 – 21	F
20 – 15	G
Below 15	U

20 - 16 marks Answers will contain a majority of these points:
- *the piece is presented as an article, such as adding a headline*
- *further evidence of the piece being an article in the tone or style – friendly but not too informal*
- *good structure to the piece, working sensibly through a number of points*
- *sensible ideas showing some of the problems and ideas for solutions*
- *reference to the school but not rambling inappropriate details*
- *good expression, varied and interesting to read*
- *at the top end of this band, work is technically very good with few errors in punctuation and spelling, at the bottom end there are a few errors in common words.*

15 - 11 marks Answers will contain a majority of these points:
- *some sense of the piece being an article, such as a headline*
- *tone is less certain than top band work although evidence of a newspaper style*
- *some solutions as well as the problems*
- *they keep close to the brief although some comments or ideas may be superficial*
- *expression is fair but sometimes repetitive*
- *work is technically fair but common and repeated errors in the lower part of this band, particularly in punctuation.*

10 - 6 marks Answers will contain a majority of these points:
- *the article might appear more like an essay*
- *there may be too many problems mentioned without solutions or*
- *brief references to solutions, some might be inappropriate*
- *sense of rushed or unplanned work*
- *expression is limited in places or inappropriate choice of words.*

USED CARS
A GUIDE FOR PEOPLE WHO KNOW LITTLE ABOUT THEM

Before Buying

Buying a used car isn't as simple as buying other things. Make a mistake and you could lose a lot of money or have a nasty accident. Or both.

You can be ripped off in lots of ways. If you can't tell a poor bargain from a sound buy, this leaflet tries to help you. It covers buying **privately,** from a **dealer** or at an **auction.** It also tells you how to get your car properly **serviced.**

Even if car engines and bodywork are a complete mystery, you can help yourself in several ways. When you know the type and age of the car you want and have a rough idea of how much you can afford:

- find out what the insurance will cost. Ask several firms. If you are under 25 or if you want a fast car, you may be regarded as a bad risk and have to pay a hefty premium.
- think about servicing and repair costs. Is there a local dealer?
- remember MOT test certificates (£29). All cars must have one when they are over three years old. Will your car pass?
- check whether the car has seat belts for rear passengers.

Buying privately

If you buy privately take as much care as when buying from a dealer – but make some extra checks.

Does the person selling the car really own it? It could be stolen! Insist on seeing the vehicle registration document, and check that the seller's name and address is on it. Ask the seller to prove his or her identity.

Make sure you discuss the deal at the seller's home. Does he or she really live there? You might have trouble with the car and want to get in touch again.

If the car is more than three years old, make sure it has an MOT test certificate. But you still need to have the car checked by an expert. The car passed some basic tests on the day, but serious faults could exist.

Check car prices in a used-car guide. A private seller doesn't have the expenses of a dealer so aim to pay less.

If you buy privately, the car must be as described by the seller. So make a note of anything said about the car, and keep a copy of any advertisement. Try to get the seller to describe the car in writing. This could be very important if you have trouble with the vehicle.

Because they know the law is different for private sales, some dealers try to cheat you of your legal rights by pretending to be private sellers. They advertise in shop windows and in local newspapers, just as you'd sell a pram. Beware of people who insist on meeting you anywhere, except at their own homes. Be on your guard if the same phone number crops up again and again. If the seller's name and address is not on the vehicle registration document, he or she could be a dealer.

Used Cars

Buying from a dealer

**Take care in selecting a dealer.
Check whether the garage is a member of one of the four trade associations which have a code of practice intended to help you.
Look for the signs on the right:**

See whether your friends have any ideas. Find someone who seems to be well regarded and has proper premises. Look for a garage whose cars have already been inspected by the AA or RAC.

Some dealers pretend to be private owners. They want to cheat you of your legal rights if anything goes wrong with the car so avoid them. (See BUYING PRIVATELY.)

Don't be in a hurry to buy. Shop around. Compare prices of cars of the same age and condition. You can buy used-car price guides in newsagents.

**Is there a warranty (or guarantee)? What does it include?
If it covers mechanical breakdown for two or three years, make sure that it's in the form of an insurance policy (otherwise it might be worthless). Do you have to pay extra for it? If so, how much?**

Try haggling over the price.

If the salesman talks jargon tell him to explain things simply.

Unless you are an expert, you take a risk if you buy a car that hasn't been checked and road tested by a mechanic or engineer. The AA and RAC will check a car for you - for a fee. Some dealers - and private sellers! - fiddle the mileage reading on the clock so, for example, it shows 40,000 instead of 80,000. This is 'clocking'. It is illegal, but it happens. Be wary if a dealer won't guarantee the mileage. He may have tried to check it and failed - or he may suspect it has been clocked.

Ask for a vehicle registration document. It gives the number of owners (called 'keepers') and the name and address of the last one. Contact the last owner to see whether the mileage is correct.

On average a private car does about 8,000 miles a year. A company car will do a lot more. Does the car's general condition match up with the mileage?

Car Auctions
If you are thinking of looking for a bargain at a car auction, make sure you know what you are doing. It would be a good idea to take an expert along with you if you don't know much about cars. First, go as a spectator and see what happens. Study the auctioneer's conditions of business.

Foundation Level – Questions

Used Cars

Time: _____

Read all of 'Used Cars' before you answer the questions.

1. Using **only** the section called 'Before Buying', say what expenses will be involved in **running** a car?
   (3 marks)

2. Using **only** the section called 'Buying from a dealer', give three useful checks you should make before choosing a garage to buy from.
   (3 marks)

3. What is a 'clocked' car and how can you check to see if a car has been 'clocked'?
   (4 marks)

4. Why might a dealer try to sell a car from a private address? Describe two ways of telling if someone is a dealer and not a private seller.
   (4 marks)

5. Using **only** the section called 'Before Buying', explain four ways that the style of the leaflet tries to make the information clear and easy to follow.
   (4 marks)

6. Why do you think the leaflet uses so many questions? Is this a helpful or unhelpful way of presenting information?
   (4 marks)

Choose one of the following questions:

7a. A friend of yours is planning to buy a used car and is looking for advice. Write a letter offering advice on what to look out for and what to be careful of. Use material from 'Used Cars' to help you but avoid merely copying.
   (20 marks)

   or

7b. Joe has seen a car that appears to be a good bargain in the small ads in the local newspaper. He doesn't know that the seller (Mr. Edwards) is a dealer. Joe has read the information booklet. Write, as a script, the telephone conversation between the two. You can decide if Joe makes good use of the advice from the booklet.
   (20 marks)

Used Cars

Foundation Level – Answers

Used Cars Marking Suggestions

Advised Time: 60 minutes

1. Using **only** the section called 'Before Buying', say what expenses will be involved in **running** a car? *(3 marks)*
   - cost of the insurance
   - servicing / repair costs
   - MOT test

   Do not award marks for information not on the page or mis-reading the question such as cost of buying the car or petrol.

2. Using **only** the section called Buying from a dealer', give three useful checks you should make before choosing a garage to buy from. *(3 marks)*
   One for each point up to a maximum of three:
   - the garage is a member of a trade association
   - the garage has proper premises
   - cars are AA / RAC inspected
   - compare prices of cars
   - use a price guide.

3. What is a 'clocked' car and name two ways you can check to see if a car has been 'clocked'? *(4 marks)*
   - 'clocked' means that the mileage reading has been tampered with to lower the mileage shown *(2 marks)*
   One for each reason, up to a maximum of two:
   - ask to see the vehicle registration document (and then contact the previous owner)
   - ask the dealer to guarantee the mileage

4. Why might a dealer try to sell a car from a private address? Describe two ways of telling if someone is a dealer and not a private seller. *(4 marks)*
   - the law is different if dealers sell from a private address and they have less legal responsibilities if the car goes wrong *(2 marks)*
   One mark for each way, up to a maximum of two:
   - the dealer may not sell the car at their home address
   - there may be many cars advertised with the same phone number
   - the seller's name is not on the Vehicle Registration document.

5. Using **only** the section called 'Before Buying', explain four ways that the style of the leaflet tries to make the information clear and easy to follow. *(4 marks)*
   - the language is simple and clearly expressed
   - short sentences are used to break up the information
   - slang / 'chatty' terms are used e.g. 'you can be ripped off', 'a rough idea.'
   - certain words are highlighted.

6. Why do you think the leaflet asks so many questions? Is this a helpful or unhelpful way of presenting information?
   (Up to a maximum of 4 marks)
   - it asks questions to get the reader and possible buyer to think about all the different aspects of buying a car *(2 marks)*
   - it's helpful as it involves the reader, they have to respond to what they are reading *(2 marks)*
   - it could be seen as unhelpful as there are a lot of questions and the reader might miss one or get confused.

   An answer that combines these points or gives other sensible justifications should also earn up to four marks.

7a. A friend of yours is planning to buy a used car and is looking for advice. Write a letter offering advice on what to look out for and what to be careful of. *(20 marks)*

20 – 15 marks Answers will contain a majority of these points:
   - proper letter layout
   - opening paragraph that sets the context/ explains the purpose for writing
   - suitable tone as it is a close friend, friendly and chatty
   - information about type, size of car and possible price
   - good use of the advice from the booklet. Information is summarised and main points included. Very little, if any, is copied word for word
   - a good structure to the piece
   - good use of the time so the piece is of a reasonable length and finished properly
   - technically very good at the top end with few errors. Errors in spelling / punctuation pull the overall mark to the lower end of this band.

14 – 9 marks Answers will contain a majority of these points:
   - proper letter layout
   - a brief explanation of why they are writing
   - suitable tone although they are likely to adopt the more formal tone of the booklet

Foundation Level – Answers — Used Cars

- a good number of points chosen from the booklet. Some of the information may be copied or very similar in wording but
- points may be randomly assembled and not in the best order
- evidence of less structure to the overall piece e.g. a rushed ending
- technically fair but there may be common and repeated errors.

Two Notes:
1. Lower marks for not mentioning the type of car or too much detail about the car to the detriment of giving advice
2. Penalise mis-spellings of words that are in the booklet.

8 – 4 marks Answers will contain a majority of these points:
- some form of letter layout
- abrupt opening or too much time spent on pleasantries
- not mentioning the type of car or too much detail about the car to the detriment of giving advice
- advice is presented poorly, probably without explanation or it may be misleading, the advice is likely to jump from point to point
- limited range of expression
- technically weak although the mistakes do not hamper the overall meaning.

7b. Joe has seen a car that appears to be a good bargain in the small ads in the local newspaper. He doesn't know that the seller (Mr. Edwards) is a dealer. Joe has read the information booklet. Write, as a script, the telephone conversation between the two. You can decide if Joe makes good use of the advice from the booklet.
(20 marks)

20 – 15 marks Answers will contain a majority of these points:
- a script layout, it is clear who is speaking
- a suitable opening such as Joe explaining who he is and why he is phoning
- evidence of Edwards being deceptive about being a dealer
- Joe making good use of the booklet's advice such as asking appropriate questions
- progression in the conversation, they do not linger on the same points
- a good structure to the piece
- good use of the time so the piece is of a reasonable length and finished properly
- technically very good at the top end with few errors. Errors in spelling / punctuation pull the overall mark to the lower end of this band.

14 – 9 marks Answers will contain a majority of these points:
- a script layout, it is usually clear who is speaking
- some explanation as to why Joe is phoning
- evidence of Edwards being deceptive about being a dealer although in this band it is more obviously shown / less subtle
- Joe asks a reasonable number of questions although they are not always in the best order
- responses from the two speakers are likely to be brief and direct, less range of expression
- at the lower end of this band the piece may be repetitive or brief
- evidence of less structure to the overall piece e.g. a rushed ending
- technically fair but there may be common and repeated errors.

8 – 4 marks Answers will contain a majority of these points:
- a script layout, it is usually clear who is speaking
- some explanation as to why Joe is phoning
- ideas may be copied word for word from the booklet, or
- much more information needs to be taken from the booklet
- responses from the two speakers are likely to be very brief and direct, a limited range of expression
- the piece is repetitive and / or brief
- technically weak although the mistakes do not hamper the overall meaning.

Two notes:
1. An answer that fails to use the script layout, e.g. the piece is written as a story, should be severely penalised.
2. Speech marks for scripts are not needed. Marks should not be deducted for use of speech marks unless they hamper the reading and understanding.

Guide to grade boundaries	
42 – 37	C
36 – 31	D
30 – 25	E
24 – 19	F
18 – 13	G
Below 13	U

The Cost of a Drink

> A YOUNG MAN was killed and his passenger seriously injured when their car ploughed into a traffic island on Grange Road late on Monday night.
> Michael Crawshaw, 21, and Susan Crosby, 19, were rushed to Victoria Hospital. The man died shortly afterwards in Casualty. Miss Crosby's condition was described as 'serious'.
> Police said that no other vehicles were involved and that the cause had yet to be established, although alcohol had not been ruled out.

"We just can't believe it. Michael was always such a careful driver."

I just knew something was wrong when the doorbell went at two in the morning. I said to Jack, 'Oh no, something's happened to Michael.' I couldn't help hoping the Police had got it wrong, that it was someone else, not my boy. I knew the moment I saw the doctor. His eyes turned away and I knew. It didn't hit us straight away, but all we've got now is the memories. I keep thinking about the poor girl. We hardly even knew her, we'd seen her just the once. She seemed very nice. We both desperately want to do something to help but, well, where do you start?"

"The public just don't realise how many people get hurt."

Joe and me, we got there at around ten to midnight, not long after the crash. From the state of the Capri, the lad must have been doing a fair lick, maybe 40 or 45. You could tell from the tyre marks he'd lost control about 15 yards before the traffic island. Look, the facts are all in the official report. But you won't find the whole story there. The truth is we're used to all the tricks. Drivers who've had one or two. They'll try anything. You know, dodging down the back roads - as if we didn't know about them. Well, this lad won't be worrying about that any more. Or about the mess he's left behind. It's the girl I feel sorry for. She's the one who's got to live with it. It won't be much of a life, will it?"

The Cost of a Drink

HOW DOES DRINKING AFFECT YOUR DRIVING?

Drinking gives a strong, but false sense of confidence.

As well as its bodily effects, it impairs your ability to judge how fit you are to drive.

Some people believe, wrongly, that they drive better after a few drinks.

Young and inexperienced drivers are more seriously impaired well below the legal alcohol limit.

3 to 4 units make such drivers 3 times more likely to have an accident than those who have drunk no alcohol.

The legal limit for driving is 80mg of alcohol per 200ml of blood (or 107mg/100ml of urine). In the breath, it is 35 micrograms (µg) per 100ml.

Even a small amount of alcohol can affect your driving. The only safe way is not to drink and drive.

WHAT DOES DRINKING AND DRIVING REALLY COST?

Over a thousand people are killed each year as a result of drinking and driving, many of them innocent victims.

For every one killed, a lot more are injured, some permanently disabled. Still more are badly affected among the victims' families and friends.

Well over half the drivers and riders killed on weekend nights (Fridays and Saturdays) are over the legal alcohol limit.

The cost in human suffering is beyond measure. The legal penalties, however, are quite clear.

There is a minimum 1 year's disqualification with a fine of up to £2,000 and/or prison.

Travel becomes difficult and expensive; so does getting insurance at the end of a ban. Professional drivers may even lose their jobs and income.

HOW DOES ALCOHOL AFFECT YOUR BODY?

Alcohol is a drug which takes effect quickly, but wears off slowly.

It takes just 20 minutes to act, less on an empty stomach.

It passes into the bloodstream and all around the body, including the brain.

Alcohol lessens muscular co-ordination and slows down reactions. It blurs vision and decreases awareness.

The body eliminates alcohol at the rate of 1 unit an hour.

Even sleeping for 8 hours only removes the alcohol from four pints of ordinary beer

Coffee may wake you up slightly, but that's all. The popular stories about peppermints and painkillers are just myths.

Nothing can remove alcohol from the blood, except time.

The Cost of a Drink

YOUR PRACTICAL GUIDE TO CRIME PREVENTION

Alcohol and drugs

Most people are aware that drinking to excess can damage their health.

There is also a clear link between excessive drinking and certain types of crime. Some offences are alcohol-related by definition – drink-driving – for example. But these are by no means the only ones in which alcohol plays a large part. Public disorder, including football hooliganism and vandalism is particularly associated with it. There is also an indirect link, in that alcohol abuse may create the sort of unhappy family from which children are more likely to turn to crime.

Drinking and driving

Alcohol is a major cause of accidents on the road. One in five drivers killed in road accidents have drunk more than the legal limit for driving. The legal limit is 80 milligrams of alcohol in 100 millilitres of blood. But there is no sure way of telling how much you can drink before you reach this limit. It varies with each person depending on weight, your sex, whether you've just eaten and what sort of drinks you've had.

• Your driving ability can be affected by just one or two drinks even if you are below the legal limit, you can still be prosecuted if a police officer considers your driving has been affected by alcohol.

• The best advice is **never** drink and drive.

Alcohol and your children

Young people, like adults, need to know how to drink safely. By the time they reach their teens, many will be drinking socially at parties, clubs and discos. Although most do so sensibly, a number come to harm through excessive drinking.

The risk is that, as inexperienced drinkers, young people may make mistakes about when and how much is safe to drink. Heavy drinking and drunkenness are more common in the late teens and early twenties than in any other age group.

Their chances of coming to harm - hangovers and sickness, fights, trouble with the police and accidents resulting in injury or even death - are that much greater.

Here is some advice to help protect your children from these dangers:

• Set a good example by drinking sensibly yourself. Children pick up their early knowledge of alcohol by watching adults and are strongly influenced by what they see.

• Alcohol is often shown in a glamorous light. Point out that it has a negative as well as a positive side, and that it is not essential to socialising and having fun.

• Try to explain to your children why you want them to understand alcohol and drink sensibly. Try to discuss the subject, and to understand their views as well as putting your own.

• Tell them it is alright to stop when they have had enough, or to have a soft drink. Encourage them to choose low alcohol rather than stronger drinks. Tell them they shouldn't mix strong drinks.

• Warn them of the risks. Drunkenness can lead to arguments, fights and trouble with the police. Discourage them from drinking in the street, especially in groups, as this can be intimidating to other people.

• Remind them that driving is much more dangerous after any amount of alcohol.

- Make a drink-and-drive pact with your children
- Ask your children to agree:
  - Never to drink alcohol if they intend to drive
  - Never to accept a lift from someone who's been drinking
  - To call a cab which you (parents) will pay for if they can't use public transport to get home.

Foundation Level – Questions

The Cost of a Drink

Time: _____

Read 'The Cost of a Drink' and 'Alcohol and Drugs', and then answer the questions.

1. Name three alcohol related crimes.   *(3 marks)*

2. What age group is most likely to be involved in heavy drinking and drunkenness?
   (2 marks)

3. According to the reading materials, what can be the consequences of drunken driving? (Explain in your own words)   *(5 marks)*

4. 'Your Practical Guide to Crime Prevention' is written for parents. Do you feel it gives good advice and is it well-explained? Explain your reasons.
   (5 marks)

5. Look at what Michael's parents say and what the police say. Explain the differences between the way the parents and police report the incident. Pay close attention to the language.   *(5 marks)*

Choose one of the following questions to answer:

6a. Alcohol drinking is a way of life and the more you restrict it the more likely it is that there will be underage drinkers. What are your views on this issue? Present both sides of the argument in the form of a script, perhaps like a debate on television.   *(20 marks)*

or

6b. The local youth club needs a hard-hitting campaign to warn of the dangers of drinking and they have asked you to get it organised. They want to know your ideas and how you might organise an evening for other teenagers to present this issue. Explain your ideas and what you plan to do.
   (20 marks)

The Cost of a Drink — Foundation Level – Answers

The Cost of a Drink Marking Suggestions   **Advised Time: 60 minutes**

1. Name three alcohol related crimes. *(3 marks)*
   - *drink driving*
   - *vandalism*
   - *hooliganism*

2. What age group is most likely to be involved in heavy drinking and drunkenness? *(2 marks)*
   - **Late teens and early 20's**

3. According to the reading materials, what can be the consequences of drunken driving? (Explain in your own words) *(1 for each, 5 maximum)*
   - *innocent people killed*
   - *innocent people injured*
   - *some may be permanently disabled*
   - *friends of the victims are scarred too*
   - *driving disqualification*
   - *prison*
   - *lose your job*
   - *difficult to get insurance.*

4. 'Your Practical Guide to Crime Prevention' is written for parents. Do you feel it gives good advice and is it well-explained? Explain your reasons. *(5 marks)*
   Some of the strengths of the article (make sure they keep to the article)
   - *article breaks down the topic into paragraphs and then into bullet points.*
   - *explanation is in short clear sentences*
   - *concludes with six or more tips and advice*
   - *article 'accepts' that young people do drink and advises moderation*
   - *a few facts support the arguments*

   A justified comment with an example that argues that the article is not well-explained or gives confusing advise should gain two marks.

5. Look at what Michael's parents say and what the police say. Explain the differences between the way the parents and police report the incident. Pay close attention to the language.
   (5 marks, at least two points from each)
   Police
   - *report it as an everyday fact, there is less emotion*
   - *familiarity with the incident*
   - *fairly impersonal about those involved, just referred to as 'boy' and 'girl'*
   - *more detail about the car and what it did*
   - *use of slang – 'lad', 'fair lick'.*

   Parents
   - *describes the people, driver is named*
   - *others' emotions and how it affected them*
   - *sense of helplessness 'where do you start?'*
   - *their account is a rambling collection of emotions.*

6a. Alcohol drinking is a way of life and the more you restrict it the more likely it is that there will be underage drinkers. What are your views on this issue? Present both sides of the argument in the form of a script, like a debate on television.
   20 – 15 marks Answers will contain a majority of these points:
   - *well-organised work that has shown some planning*
   - *the debate should have an introduction, even if it is a short factual one*
   - *reference to the information in the resource material*
   - *views are justified and explained*
   - *good points made for both sides of the argument*
   - *discussion keeps close to the question set*
   - *technically good at the top end of the band, few errors with common words and punctuation at the bottom of this band.*

   14 – 9 marks Answers will contain a majority of these points:
   - *good ideas that are unlikely to be in the best order*
   - *ideas may not be explained or justified*
   - *likely to be an unbalanced argument*
   - *some reference to the resource material*
   - *work is technically fair but common and repeated errors in the lower part of this band, particularly in punctuation.*

   8 – 4 marks Answers will contain a majority of these points:
   - *the piece has been hastily planned*
   - *it may not be in script form as requested*
   - *views presented haphazardly and with little justification*
   - *technically weak although the mistakes do not hamper the overall meaning.*

Foundation Level – Answers

The Cost of a Drink

6b. The local youth club needs a hard-hitting campaign to warn of the dangers of drinking and they have asked you to get it organised. They want to know your ideas and how you might organise an evening for other teenagers to present this issue. Explain your ideas and what you plan to do.

20 –15 marks Answers will contain a majority of these points:
- *organised approach, they might detail a plan of the evening including guest speakers*
- *organisation is tied to the main topic, drinking, and not superficial matters*
- *good ideas and a recognition of the need to make it 'hard-hitting'*
- *awareness of the teenage audience, perhaps by a variety of events and suitable activities*
- *some reference to the resource material*
- *technically good at the top end of the band, few errors with common words and punctuation at the bottom of this band.*

14 – 9 marks Answers will contain a majority of these points:
- *likely to be good ideas not fully developed or explained clearly*
- *less awareness of the audience and their needs*
- *less clear that the campaign needs to be hard-hitting*
- *some reference to the resource material*
- *work is technically fair but common and repeated errors in the lower part of this band, particularly in punctuation.*

8 – 4 marks Answers will contain a majority of these points:
- *ideas randomly selected and not explained in detail, if at all*
- *ideas not likely to sustain an evening for teenagers and little understanding of 'hard-hitting'*
- *the work may show some potential but the student ran out of time before realising what he/she might contribute*
- *unlikely to be any reference to the resource material*
- *technically weak although the mistakes do not hamper the overall meaning*

Guide to grade boundaries

40 – 36	C
35 – 30	D
29 – 24	E
23 – 18	F
17 – 12	G
Below 12	U

I want my son put IN PRISON!

Jason stole his first car when he was 9. Then, at 14, he led a gang of young criminals on a crime spree. His mother Jan is at the end of her tether – but the law can't help her...

Jason hung his head in shame as his mother wept with frustration. The police had brought him home after questioning about a local burglary and, once again, the curtains were twitching across the street.

'I'm sorry, Mum, honest,' he said. 'I promise I'll stay out of trouble from now on.'

Jan shook her head in despair and disbelief. She'd heard it all before from her 14 year old son. 'I'm warning you...if you carry on like this they'll lock you up and throw away the key,' she told him.

The very next day Jason broke his promise. And another police car pulled up outside the family home in Surrey to take Jason on a route he knew only too well – to the police station.

Jan sits with her head in her hands and weeps. 'I really don't understand it,' she says. 'I brought him up to know the difference between right and wrong, and I told him that thieving was wrong. But he doesn't seem to take it in. I've tried... Oh God, how I've tried...'

But he just laughs and goes off and does it again.'

For Jan, her son's persistent offending has become a nightmare as she struggles to cope with the taunts of neighbours who blame her for her son's lawless ways. She's been forced to move home once already because of a hate campaign and now her present neighbours are turning against the family.

'I had hoped that five stretches in remand centres would have taught Jason his lesson,' says Jan, 34. 'But the regimes there were so soft, it was useless.

'I want him put somewhere tougher, like prison, in the hope it will knock some sense into him. But there's nothing the courts can do until he's older and by then it'll be too late.'

Jason hit the headlines last year when he led a gang of youths on a £2 million crime spree. They nick-named themselves the Sutton Burglary Posse, and even left calling cards for police at the scenes of their crimes.

The baby-faced mastermind had organised more than 1,000 raids on shops, businesses and banks as part of Britain's worst teenage crime wave. With seven children aged between 2 and 17 at home, single mum Jan often finds the pressure too much to bear.

'I cry myself to sleep,' she says. 'Jason has broken into virtually every house in the district, and I can't even walk to the shops with my younger children without getting abuse hurled at me.

'But I've done everything I can to keep him on the straight and narrow... I've followed him to school to make sure he wasn't playing truant, and I've tried to stop him seeing friends I thought were a bad influence. Now I've come to the conclusion

I want my son put in prison

£2M CROOK AT AGE OF 14
HIS RECORD OF BREAK-INS
879 shops | 113 houses
87 motors | 4 banks

that he was born bad. Sometimes I feel I've lost the battle, but I'm determined my other children won't follow his example.'

Jason stole his first car when he was just 9. Within a few years he'd graduated to leader of the pack, turning other teenage truants into skilled burglars. Police dubbed him Kid Crook and attributed 97 per cent of raids and burglaries in the area to his gang.

'I cry myself to sleep at night'

'Jason's behaviour has got worse as he's got older,' says Jan. 'At first I'd give him a good spanking, then I tried reasoning with him...I'd tell him how much misery he'd caused whenever he broke into someone's house, and I asked him to imagine how he'd feel if his computer games or racing bike were stolen. Nothing at all worked.

'Now I'm at my wits' end. He's always promising that he'll be good, but before long the police are knocking on the door yet again...'

As a persistent offender, Jason was put under curfew and only allowed out if he was accompanied by an adult. But time and time again he's returned to a life of crime.

'The worst part is people thinking I'm a bad mother,' Jan continues. 'If I read about a 14 year old doing what he's done, I'd blame the parents, too. I'm scared he'll spend most of his adult life in jail.

By the time he was 12 he had a string of convictions – including burglaries and assaults on police officers.

'When he wasn't out causing trouble, Jason would be bunking off school. Then he started drinking – and then I found out he was smoking dope. I got leaflets on the dangers of drug-taking and stood over him while he read them. But he doesn't take any notice.
'Jason has always had plenty of cash. He bought gold chains and trainers...

He even splashed out on a string of flashy cars – despite being too young to drive.

'When he was 13, Jason went to a car showroom and paid £8,000 cash for a BMW. The salesman knew he was too young to have passed his test but he took the money.'

After Jason was caught last year, he confessed to raiding 879 shops and businesses in his home town, plus 113 houses and four banks. The stiffest penalty he could receive was a 12 month supervision order. At the time, Home Office Minister David MacLean said: 'The present position, where we can't have persistent criminals under the age of 15 detained, is ridiculous. We'll put a stop to this as soon as the law is approved.'

Jason is still free to roam the streets and he has no intention of giving up his life of crime. 'Once I learned how easy it was to get into shops, I was hooked' he says.

The Criminal Justice and Public Order Act, which became

law in November 1994, extended the courts' powers to deal with young offenders. But the secure training centres, where juveniles will be detained, have yet to be built.

Det Sgt Kevin Choules of Epsom Divisional Burglary Squad, which patrols Sutton, says: 'The way things stand there's not a lot we or the courts can do. But when we do arrest the main ringleaders and detain them for any length of time, there's a significant decrease in crime figures. I've no doubt if we could get a custodial sentence, it would cut crime on the streets.'

'He always promises he'll be good'

For Jan, the new regulations have come too late. 'Maybe if his first brush with the law had made him respect the courts a bit more, he wouldn't be looking at an adult life behind bars,' she says.

'I want to apologise to everyone he's burgled but, most of all, I'd like to see him apologise. I want to believe it's not too late for him to change...'

£2M FOR KICKS
Supercrook's stomping ground: stores robbed by the young tearaway in Sutton High Street
SUTTON

Woman's Own,
Mark Christy
- Press Gang News

I want my son put in prison

Foundation Level – Questions

Time: _____

Read 'I want my son put in prison' and then answer the questions.

1. Name three different crimes that Jason has committed.
   (3 marks)

2. What has Jason's mother done to try to stop her son's criminal behaviour?
   (6 marks)

3. Explain why Jason has not been sent to prison.
   (2 marks)

4a. Why do you think, '*I want my son put in prison*' is an effective eye-catching title?
   (2 marks)

4b. Is there anything else in the presentation of this article that makes it eye-catching?
   (4 marks)

5. Do you feel the article would encourage or deter other young offenders? Explain your reasons.
   (3 marks)

Choose one of the following questions to answer:

6a. Imagine you are Jason and are being held in a remand centre.
   Write a letter to your mother that explains why you lead such a criminal life.
   (20 marks)

   or

6b. The police wish to start a campaign in your school, aimed at Year 7, to stop young people breaking the law. Offer the police some advice on how they could start the campaign and make it effective. You could present this as a letter or a report.
   (20 marks)

Foundation Level – Answers

I want my son put in prison

I want my son put in prison Marking Suggestions   **Advised Time: 75 minutes**

1. Name three different crimes that Jason has committed.
   (1 for each up to 3 maximum)
   - *raids on shops, banks, businesses*
   - *broken into houses*
   - *drug taking*
   - *stealing cars*
   - *truanting*
   - *hit a police officer.*

2. What has Jason's mother done to try to stop her son's criminal behaviour?
   (1 for each up to 6 maximum)
   - *told him off*
   - *tried to show him right from wrong*
   - *reasoned with him*
   - *followed him to school so he doesn't truant*
   - *stopped him seeing bad friends*
   - *spanked him when younger*
   - *put under curfew*
   - *shown him leaflets on drug taking.*

3. Explain why Jason has not been sent to prison. *(2 marks)*
   - *he is too young as they cannot take persistent offenders under 15.*

4a. Why do you think, 'I want my son put in prison' is an effective eye-catching title? *(2 marks)*
   - *it is not what a mother would normally ask to happen to her children.*

4b. Is there anything else in the presentation of the article that makes it eye-catching? *(4 marks)*
   - *the sub headline with the amazing facts*
   - *the press cuttings with their prominent headlines*
   - *picture of the mother where she doesn't show her face*
   - *the dramatic quotations breaking up the text.*

   The emphasis should be on layout and not content of the article.

5. Do you feel the article would encourage or deter other young offenders? Explain your reasons. *(Up to 3 marks)*
   - *Well justified reasons for deterring young people should gain full marks but the article is likely to encourage offenders because the law means they can't be imprisoned*
   - *Jason doesn't appear to have suffered much*
   - *Jason's life appears exciting, even heroic, one boy against society. His fame is even endorsed by being in this article*
   - *he has gained many material rewards but it is predicted that he will spend most of his adult life in prison*
   - *the article makes clear the effects on his mother.*

6a. Imagine you are Jason and are being held in a remand centre. Write a letter to your mother that explains why you lead such a criminal life.

20 – 15 marks Answers will contain a majority of these points:
- *proper letter layout even if the remand centre address is brief*
- *reference to some of the crimes mentioned in the article*
- *a few references to the help that the mother has given in the past*
- *letter may take a variety of tones as long as there is some consistency in attitude e.g. an arrogant defiance of authority*
- *letter keeps close to the task.*

At the top end of this band, work is technically very good with few errors in punctuation and spelling, at the bottom end there are few errors in common words.

14 – 9 marks Answers will contain a majority of these points:
- *a letter layout*
- *ideas are generally paragraphed*
- *work keeps close to the task although students may wander slightly e.g. describing the conditions of the remand centre*
- *reference to a few of the crimes mentioned in the article*

I want my son put in prison
Foundation Level – Answers

- work is technically fair but with common and repeated errors in the lower part of this band, particularly in punctuation.

8 – 4 marks Answers will contain a majority of these points:
- the piece has been hastily planned and written with ideas not presented in the best order and it is unlikely to be paragraphed
- technically weak although the mistakes do not hamper the overall meaning.

Note: Some students might include deliberate errors (Jason has, after all, truanted a great deal) or a deliberately inconsistent attitude, showing mixed feelings. This will require careful weighing by the marker.

6b. The police wish to start a campaign in your school, aimed at Year 7, to stop young people breaking the law. Offer the police some advice on how they could start the campaign and make it effective. You could present this as a letter or a report.

20 – 15 marks Answers will contain a majority of these points:
- well organised work that has shown some planning
- some reference to the article showing the problems crime causes for a family
- reasons justified and explained
- awareness of the audience the police will be working with and some ideas on how to interest younger students.

At the top end of this band, work is technically very good with few errors in punctuation and spelling, at the bottom end there are few errors in common words.

14 – 9 marks Answers will contain a majority of these points:
- some good ideas that are unlikely to be in the best order
- some ideas may not be explained or justified
- less sensitivity about the age of the audience
- work is technically fair but common and repeated errors in the lower part of this band, particularly in punctuation.

8 – 4 marks Answers will contain a majority of these points:
- the piece has been hastily planned and written with ideas not presented in the best order and it is unlikely to be paragraphed
- technically weak although the mistakes do not hamper the overall meaning.

Guide to grade boundaries		
40	- 36	C
35	- 30	D
29	- 24	E
23	- 18	F
17	- 12	G
Below 12		U

117 Days Adrift

Maurice and Maralyn Bailey planned to sail the world in their yacht, Auralyn. One month into their crossing of the Pacific Ocean their boat is holed by a whale. As their boat sinks, they make their escape into a small life raft and rubber dinghy.

The first extract describes the day of the sinking.

Maurice   March 4th

Auralyn had finally disappeared and we felt very much alone in that wide ocean. There was nothing left to show her going but the loose equipment that had floated free. Neither of us spoke: each left the other alone with their thoughts. Maralyn kept herself busy by putting the raft in some sort of order, whilst I rowed the dinghy amongst the debris and retrieved four containers of water, one of kerosene and one of methylated spirits (alcohol). Rowing over to the raft I made the dinghy fast with two twenty-five foot lines and then paid out the sea-anchor and made that fast to the raft. My movements were slow and laborious, mentally I was in a state of shock and low spirits.

I rested and looked across at Maralyn. She was weeping. For the first time in my life I felt utter despair, utter helplessness.

'We're near a shipping lane,' I said with a confidence I did not feel. 'We'll be seen soon.'

Maralyn stopped her work and looked up and said softly, 'I was planning to have a plaque engraved in New Zealand, saying thank you to Auralyn for carrying us so safely, and to fix it to the main hatch.' She paused and then said, 'It has all gone ... everything we have worked for ... now we have nothing.'

It was heartbreaking. Auralyn had been more than just a boat to us, she had been a friend and companion - our home.

There was no recrimination. Maralyn was wonderful. She did not blame me for our desperate plight. Yet I blamed myself and I probed my mind to find exactly what I had done wrong. Was there something more that I could have done to have saved the ship? Everything appeared confused just before we abandoned Auralyn and now with the clarity generated from hindsight I imagined that, with a little more effort, I could have saved her. I think that I was mistaken, nothing could have saved that boat.

Maralyn broke into my thoughts, 'What do you think of our chances?' she asked. I felt that I must give her hope.

'Fairly good,' I said. 'How much food and water have we got?'

'Enough for twenty days, with careful rationing,' she replied.

'Give us another ten days without food and water, we could last for thirty days,' I said with false jubilance. 'Surely, someone is bound to see us within four weeks.'

117 Days Adrift

The second extract comes from 93 days later. They have still not been seen or rescued. Maurice is in the dinghy which is tied to the life raft in the middle of a violent storm.

Maralyn   June 5th (Day 93)

I had felt myself going up as if in a lift and realised that I was on the crest of a huge wave. I gazed at the dinghy below me and suddenly the raft began charging down the face of the wave towards it. I expected them to crash together and braced myself for the impact but before I reached it the dinghy was flying in the air and disappeared in a smother of foam.

Unable to speak or do anything, I gazed at the upturned dinghy. I can hardly describe my relief when I saw Maurice's head break the surface behind the dinghy. It took many minutes of combined effort before he was 'landed' in the raft. As he rested I turned my attention to the dinghy and watched a plastic container go scudding by, just out of reach.

The oars, water carriers and compass were tied to the dinghy so before we could right it we had to fumble to undo the fastenings and bring as much as we could into the raft. Then began the herculean task of turning the dinghy over. Several times we almost succeeded when the wind caught it and pulled it away from our grasp and it flopped once more face down on the sea. Finally, we managed to right it and lash everything back in place. We were both exhausted by our efforts and, as we lay resting, we took stock of our position. Our bait had disappeared and also all our fishing gear.

Maurice

That night it was impossible to sleep; waves buffeted the raft and constantly moved our equipment from its various stowed positions. We spent much of our time restowing everything. Occasionally, a wave would strike us hard and water would splash up the canopy and cascade into the raft. Then we would have to bale furiously. This always dismayed us because salt water on the canopy meant that we needed much rain in the future to clean the salt away before it could be used for drinking. Rarely did we manage to get the water below the level of our hips. Our legs, thighs and buttocks were being continually chafed on the black rubber adding to our discomfort. Because of the deep, ulcer-like sores on my rump and hips it was impossible to find a comfortable position for my body.

Suddenly, as though we had been struck by some giant's hammer, we found ourselves climbing violently towards the vertical, propelled by a blow from a wave that broke right over us. The entrance flap burst open and a mass of water exploded into the raft. After the torrent of water had stopped and we had realised that the raft was still upright, we began the tormenting task of emptying the raft once more.

Maralyn and I looked towards each other in the blackness of the night as we sat back, tired out with our efforts.

'What will happen if the raft capsizes?' Maralyn asked. I was angry at this question because I did not know the answer. Surely she can work it out for herself, I thought, but, perhaps, it is just reassurance she needs.

I said, 'I don't think it will capsize, but we must prepare ourselves for that to happen. Get what is left of the tinned food, the knives and tin opener and put them all into the haversack.'

We groped in the darkness and placed everything we could find inside the haversack we had used for our emergency pack. Then Maralyn found a piece of cord and lashed it to the raft.

'If the raft goes over at least we shall be able to save those few things,' I said. 'It will be very difficult to right it in these seas.'

'I don't feel like dying, not tonight anyway,' Maralyn said, feeling for my hand. It was then, I think, that I fully appreciated the extent of Maralyn's tenacity for life; it would not be any failing on her part if we did not survive.

The storm lasted for four days during which time we caught no fish and we had to use our precious supply of canned food. Fresh bait would now be essential before we could start fishing again.

Taken from 117 Days Adrift by Maurice and Maralyn Bailey, The Nautical Printing Company

Foundation Level – Questions

117 Days Adrift

Time: _____

Read both extracts before answering the questions.

1. Name two items that they have managed to rescue from their yacht.
   (2 marks)

2. Give two reasons why Maralyn might be keeping herself busy.
   (2 marks)

3. In the first extract Maurice and Maralyn are trying to stay confident about being rescued. Give two facts they mention and two opinions.
   (4 marks)

4. In the second extract, which is the worst moment of the storm for the Baileys? *(2 marks)*

5. *'What will happen if the raft capsizes?'* Maralyn asked
   What is the answer that Maurice knows but doesn't give?
   Why doesn't he answer it? *(2 marks)*

6. What are the advantages of this story being told by the people who it happened to? Refer closely to the passages to explain your reasons.
   (4 marks)

7. Apart from the raft overturning, mention five other problems the couple face during the storm. *(5 marks)*

8. Do you think Maralyn has the same view about the situation they are in, at the start and 93 days later? Support your view with ideas or quotations from both extracts. *(4 marks)*

Choose one of the following questions:

9a. Imagine you are a radio reporter for the Southampton News and are able to interview Maurice and Maralyn after their safe return.
In script form, write your radio interview with them, asking about their ordeal.
Try to use details from the extracts for some of the interview.
(20 marks)

9b. Do you think people are foolish to take on risky journeys? Is there any value in taking on something dangerous? Use the extract, anything you've heard about in the news and your own ideas to discuss these questions. *(20 marks)*

9c. Imagine you are either Maurice or Maralyn and have been stranded at sea for 45 days. Write your diary for the day. Try to make use of the information from the extracts. *(20 marks)*

117 Days Adrift Marking Suggestions

Advised Time: 75 minutes

1. Name two items that they have managed to rescue from their yacht. *(2 marks)*
   Any two-
   - *four containers of water*
   - *kerosene container*
   - *methylated spirits container.*

2. Give two reasons why Maralyn might be keeping herself busy. *(2 marks)*
   - *sort out what they have*
   - *see what they have left after the sinking so as not to think about the disaster.*

3. In the first extract Maurice and Maralyn are trying to stay confident about being rescued. Give two facts they mention and two opinions. *(4 marks)*
   - *(Fact) We're near a shipping lane*
   - *(Fact) Enough food for twenty days*

   Any two of these:
   - *(Opinion) We could last for thirty days*
   - *(Opinion) We'll be seen soon or Someone is bound to see us within four weeks*
   - *(Opinion) Maurice says their chances are fairly good.*

4. In the second extract, which is the worst moment of the storm for the Baileys? *(2 marks)*
   - *'as though we had been struck by some giant hammer.' When a wave blows over the craft, the entrance hatch bursts open and a torrent of water bursts in.*

5. 'What will happen if the raft capsizes?' Maralyn asked. What is the answer that Maurice knows but doesn't give? Why doesn't he answer it? *(2 marks)*
   - *if the raft capsizes they will probably drown*
   - *he wants to reassure Maralyn so he says it probably won't turn over.*

6. What are the advantages of this story being told by the people who it happened to? Refer closely to the passages to explain your reasons. *(4 marks)*
   The two key facts are below, one mark for each plus one mark for each piece of evidence that supports this, up to four marks.
   - *Adds realism as the people actually experienced it and they can describe their feelings. e.g. I had felt myself going up as if in a lift. It was then, I think, that I fully appreciated the extent of Maralyn's tenacity for life*
   - *lots of detail which you could only add if you were there. e.g. The details in securing the dinghy. The discomfort and injuries, deep, ulcer-like sores that Maurice suffered.*

7. Apart from the raft overturning, mention five other problems the couple face during the storm. *(5 marks)*
   Any five properly explained:
   - *Maurice getting into the raft*
   - *trying to turn the dinghy over*
   - *getting the equipment into the raft*
   - *they have lost their fishing gear*
   - *the raft is filling with water*
   - *their drinking supply (rain water on the canopy) is being contaminated by sea water*
   - *discomfort and sores*

8. Do you think Maralyn has the same view about the situation they are in, at the start and 93 days later? Support your view with ideas or quotations from both extracts. *(4 marks)*
   Note: Answers do not have to contain all these points, one point backed by quotation or example is worth 2 marks.
   - *Maralyn is still concerned that they may not survive the trip but she is not weeping (as she did on Day 1) and she shows fighting spirit 'I don't feel like dying, not tonight anyway' and she reassures Maurice by taking his hand*
   - *he recognises that it is through her spiritual strength that they are surviving.*

9a. Imagine you are a radio reporter for the Southampton News and are able to interview Maurice and Maralyn after their safe return. In script form, write your radio interview with them, asking them about their ordeal. Try to use details from the extracts for some of the interview.
   (20 marks)

   20 - 15 marks *Answers will contain a majority of these points:*
   - *a script layout, it is clear who is speaking*
   - *a suitable opening, such as the interviewer explaining who the people are and why they are being interviewed*
   - *good use of the extracts using details of what happened and what the Baileys felt*
   - *progression in the conversation, the best interviews will use the comments from the Baileys to lead to another question*
   - *some difference in attitude to the ordeal is shown between Maralyn and Maurice (Maralyn was far more optimistic)*
   - *a good structure to the piece*
   - *good use of the time so the piece is of a reasonable length, i.e. replies by the Baileys are not short and abrupt*
   - *technically very good, at the top end, with few errors.*

   Errors in spelling / punctuation pull the overall mark to the lower end of this band.

   14 - 9 *Answers will contain a majority of these points:*
   - *a script layout, it is usually clear who is speaking*
   - *some explanation as to why the interview is taking place*
   - *some use of the extracts although there may be an emphasis on events rather than feelings*
   - *good questions are asked although they are not in the best order and may not relate to comments from the Baileys*

Foundation Level – Answers 117 Days Adrift

- responses from the Baileys are likely to be brief and direct, less range in the expression
- evidence of less structure to the piece such as a key question being given a hasty answer
- technically fair but there may be common and repeated errors.

8 – 4 marks Answers will contain a majority of these points:
- a script layout, it is usually clear who is speaking
- some explanation as to why the interview is taking place
- comments from the Baileys may be copied word for word from the extracts or much more information needs to be taken from the extracts
- responses from the Baileys are likely to be very brief and direct, a limited range in expression.
- the piece is repetitive and/or brief
- technically weak although the mistakes do not hamper the overall meaning.

Two notes:
1. An answer that fails to use the script layout e.g. the piece is written as a story, should be severely penalised.
2. Speech marks for scripts are not needed. Marks should not be deducted for use of speech marks unless they hamper the reading and understanding.

9b. Do you think people are foolish to take on risky journeys? Is there any value in taking on something dangerous? Use the extract, anything you've heard about in the news and your own ideas to discuss these questions. *(20 marks)*

20 – 15 marks Answers will contain a majority of these points:
- well-organised work that has shown some planning
- the discussion should have an introduction, even if it is a short factual one
- reference to the information in the resource material
- at least one other reference from current or recent news about something dangerous
- views are justified and explained
- good points made for both sides of the argument
- discussion keeps close to the question set
- technically good at the top end of the band, a few errors with common words and punctuation at the bottom of this band.

14 - 9 marks Answers will contain a majority of these points:
- good ideas that are unlikely to be in the best order
- some ideas may not be explained or justified, particularly at the lower end of this band
- likely to be an unbalanced argument
- some reference to the resource material
- other references may be superficial, for example mentioning dangerous activities without drawing any suitable and thought-through conclusions from the example
- work is technically fair but common and repeated errors in the lower part of this band, particularly in punctuation.

8 - 4 marks Answers will contain a majority of these points:
- the piece has been hastily planned
- expression is weak, limited in vocabulary
- views presented haphazardly and with little justification
- unlikely to be any worthwhile use of the extracts
- technically weak although the mistakes do not hamper the overall meaning.

9c Imagine you are either Maurice or Maralyn and have been stranded at sea for 45 days. Write your diary for the day. Try to make use of the information you have read about from the extracts. *(20 marks)*

20 - 15 marks Answers will contain a majority of these points:
- the very best will attempt to adopt the style of the diary, an interesting mixture of events and feelings and
- there will be plenty of reference to the other person, particularly concerning what they may be feeling or thinking
- some empathy with their predicament, including the mixture of hope and despair, the conditions they are surviving in, their thoughts about the future
- good use of the extracts to help their ideas
- varied expression
- technically good at the top end of this band, a few errors with common words and punctuation at the bottom of this band.

14 - 9 marks Answers will contain a majority of these points:
- they have attempted to adopt the style of the diary but this may be limited by the range of expression and ideas
- they write about a number of events for the day, most are sensible and realistic, but there is less sense of understanding what it must have been like to have been stranded at sea for 45 days
- some use of the extracts to help their ideas
- work is technically fair but common and repeated errors in the lower part of this band, particularly in punctuation.

8 - 4 marks Answers will contain a majority of these points:
- the diary may be written by both people, not one as requested
- the diary is a collection of short events without reflection or feelings are superficial e.g. I was scared
- little, if any worthwhile use of the extracts
- expression is limited and repetitive
- technically weak although the mistakes do not hamper the overall expression.

Guide to grade boundaries	
45 - 40	C
39 - 34	D
33 - 28	E
27 - 22	F
21 - 16	G
Below 16	U

What's in a name?

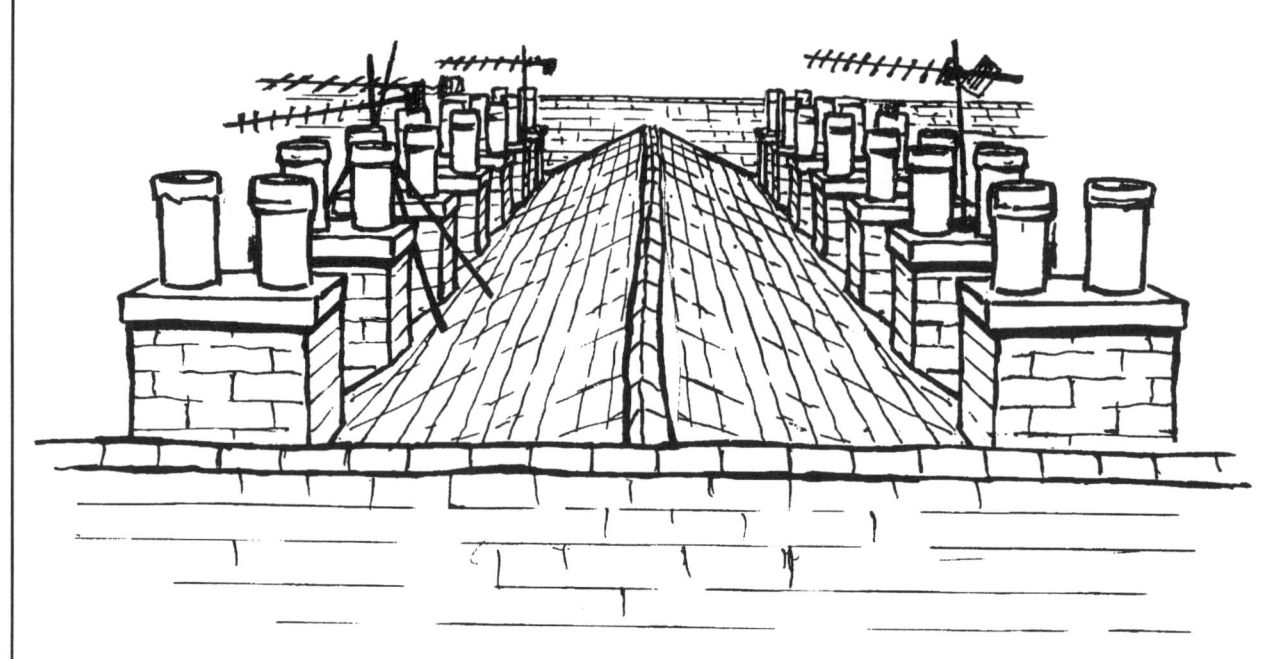

In September, millions of Coronation Street fans saw the country's most famous street turn into Cadbury's chocolate. It seems there's nowhere to hide from brand sponsorship, so says Sherry Ashworth

This article is being brought to you courtesy of Bollinger champagne, Lindt chocolates and Concorde pleasure flights. I wish.

Unfortunately, no one sponsors impecunious writers. Firms are more likely to sponsor popular television shows to get their brand name bandied about. Hence Cadbury's sweet-toothed trailer for *Coronation Street*.

There has been a tidal wave of television sponsorship recently. Continental Tyres and McDonald's are sponsoring *ITV Sports,* Del Monte are showing a fruity interest in *Gladiators,* and the weather is brought to you courtesy of Powergen, in case you were thinking it was Mother Nature.

But it doesn't really do to take the moral high ground when it comes to TV sponsorship, and especially over *Coronation Street's* lucrative relationship with Cadbury. In September, an estimated 18 million viewers watched as the *Street* was transformed into chocolate. The £10 million-partnership is the first time *Coronation Street* has been sponsored in its 35-year history. "Granada Television spent many months in discussion with a number of potential sponsors, but decided that Cadbury was the most appropriate partner to complement the heritage and traditions of the UK's most watched programme," says Andrea Wonfor of Granada.

With the help of Aardman Animation, creators of *Wallace and Gromit,* Cadbury and *Corrie* are determined to capture the audience's attention, if not make them long for a bar of chocolate. And for those viewers feeling a little irritated by the sugary prelude to each episode, the captivating sponsorship deal is also an interactive competition, offering the chance to win pots of cash with your Cadbury's bar.

The very term 'soap opera' derives from a continuing series (American), broken up into small pieces, letting soap manufacturers advertise their wares in the breaks. In those days, TV programmes really were squeaky clean. Cadbury's and *Coronation Street* are just reverting to type. Yet, we can't help but feel slightly uneasy. Adverts are boldly coming out of the closet. They are no longer confining themselves to between programmes, and are instead muscling into them. We are only a step away from a product placement. Will Curly soon be consoling himself with a box of Milk Tray? And if Prozac manufacturers take on *Eastenders,* will we at last get some upbeat storylines?

What's in a name?

Popular television programmes probably don't possess such artistic integrity that they are tainted by product placement. Even Chaucer and Shakespeare threw in the odd flattering reference to whoever happened to be their patron at the time. But there are

> **"Will Curly soon be consoling himself with a box of Milk Tray? If Prozac manufacturers take on *Eastenders*, will we at last get some upbeat storylines?"**

other, more disturbing implications of the sponsorship trend. Whoever has the money, has the power. That much is self-evident. If companies become the chief financers of television programmes, will they want to exercise a measure of control over them?

"We have absolutely no involvement with the storyline of Coronation Street from the moment it starts," says a spokesperson for Cadbury's promotion. "We just own the bit at the beginning and end."

But surely sponsors will want to choose which programmes they put their name to. It's much better to invest money in tested formulas, leaving the viewers with even more cheap, lowest-common-denominator TV, subsidised by advertisers.

I don't mind if Windowlene sponsor the weather – it is a pretty innocent sort of product. But what about the tobacco companies? At present, they're not allowed to advertise on TV. Not officially, that is. Yet turn on Formula One racing and football matches, and there are the tobacco firms plastering their brand names on hoardings everywhere.

Ordinary ads on the box clearly have a sell-by date. Repeated too often, they become hackneyed, boring even. You cry, 'I can't stand that ad,' and you go into the kitchen for a cuppa. So the advertiser has failed. Hence the development of soap-style ads like the Gold Blend saga to keep you on your seat. But TV sponsorship is one step ahead in captivating its audience. There you are all comfy in the armchair, waiting for your favourite soap, when you receive an almost subliminal plug for the product of the hour. In the case of Doritos, it's not so subliminal. Am I alone in actually having stopped buying and eating them because the sight and amplified sound of people crunching and masticating Doritos during the ITV feature film is quite sick-making.

The BBC, of course, has none of this. It exists on Government money. But for how long? Sponsorship might be the thin end of the wedge. Our present Government is always sniffing around, trying to find new ways of saving money, and there are national and multi-national companies just dying to give their money away.

And why stop at television?

Education is running short of funds too and the supermarkets have been quick to spot an opening. By saving coupons from high street supermarkets, you can help buy computer equipment for your child's school.

"We don't see the *Computers-for-Schools* scheme as replacing what the Government provides, but adding to what schools already have," argues Brigitte Burnham of Tesco's. She denied the five-year project allows the Government to abdicate its responsibility for the upkeep of school equipment.

"To date we have provided 26,000 computers for schools and 125,000 pieces of computer software. It is a way we can reward our customers for shopping with us and benefit the local community at the same time."

But come on sponsors, be more adventurous! You're already sponsoring football league tables what about the school league tables? That'll stop all those moaning minnies who say they give a distorted picture of schools' performance. Wait 'til the sponsors get hold of them. GCSE results brought to you courtesy of Heineken. And if a school is short of staff, why not ask your local employers to sponsor a teacher - she could wear a sandwich board during maths lessons and advertise your product. "Now how many packets of Strollers' cheese 'n' onion crisps does it take to fill the shelves at Bettabuys?"

> **"Why not ask your local employers to sponsor a teacher - she could wear a sandwich board during maths lessons and advertise your product"**

A nightmare indeed. Do we really want to live in a world where there's no escape from advertisers' blandishments? Sadly the audience seems utterly captive. Although it would be fun to have Virgin sponsor Paula Yates' next series...

The Big Issue

What's in a name?

Higher Level – Questions

Time: _____

Read 'What's in a name', then answer the questions.

1. Why might the writer hope that her article was being sponsored?
   (1 mark)

2. Name three programmes mentioned in the article and their sponsors.
   (3 marks)

3. What advantages are there for the Cadbury company and for Coronation Street in sponsorship?
   (2 marks)

4. Is sponsoring a new idea? Support your answer with reference to the article.
   (3 marks)

5. Is product advertising always successful? Support your answer with evidence from the article.
   (3 marks)

6. What does the writer mean by, 'Sponsorship might be the thin end of the wedge'?
   (2 marks)

7. Using the article, explain one advantage and one disadvantage of supermarkets providing computers for schools.
   (2 marks)

8. This article is written in a 'chatty' style. Name four features of this style and support each with an example.
   (8 marks)

Choose one of the following

9a. The writer suggests that a world dominated by advertising and sponsorship could be 'a nightmare'. Do you agree? Consider the writer's views as well as your own in your answer.
   (20 marks)

9b. Crunchy Crisps have written to your school offering to pay for all the student exercise books if, in return, they can put an advert for their crisps on the back cover of each book. Write two letters: the first from Crunchy Crisps to your Headteacher proposing the deal and the advantages to the school, the second letter from the Headteacher accepting or declining the offer and saying why.
   (20 marks)

9c. Sherry Ashworth's worst fears have been realised and the advertisers have taken control of Coronation Street or another soap opera of your choice. Write a few scenes in script form of this soap showing how the advertisers have muscled into the storylines.
   (20 marks)

What's in a name? Marking Suggestions

Advised Time: 90 minutes

1. Why might the writer hope that her article was being sponsored? *(1 mark)*
   - she would profit from the exotic products she mentions.

2. Name three programmes mentioned in the article and their sponsors. *(3 marks for any 3)*
   - Continental Tyres and McDonalds sponsor ITV Sports
   - Del Monte sponsors Gladiators
   - Cadbury sponsors Coronation Street
   - Powergen sponsors Weather Reports
   - Doritos sponsor the ITV feature film.

3. What advantages are there for the Cadbury company and for Coronation Street in sponsorship? *(2 marks)*
   - Coronation Street has gained around £10 million towards its production costs
   - Cadburys products will be seen by potentially 18 million viewers.

4. Is sponsoring a new idea? Support your answer with reference to the article. *(2 marks)*
   - no, Shakespeare and Chaucer also gave the occasional flattering reference to the person who paid for their writing
   - soap operas were designed to sell soap powder in the breaks.

5. Is product advertising always successful? Support your answer with evidence from the article. *(3 marks)*
   - no
   - repeated adverts make people ignore them
   - the Doritos ad has put the writer off eating them.

6. What does the writer mean by the expression, 'Sponsorship might be the thin end of the wedge'? *(2 marks for a well-explained definition)*
   - this is just a small part of a much larger problem, that is, advertising is entering many areas of our lives.

7. Using the article, explain one advantage and one disadvantage of supermarkets providing computers for schools. *(2 marks)*
   - shoppers are providing their local schools with extra equipment
   - the government may not be taking their responsibility for providing school equipment.

8. This article is written in a 'chatty' style. Name four features of this style and support each with an example. *(8 marks. One for the feature and one for the example up to 8 marks)*
   - reference to familiar products and programmes
   - short, conversational style lines e.g. I wish.
   - questions to the reader e.g. But for how long?
   - informal language e.g. But come on sponsors. That'll stop the moaning minnies.
   - abbreviated forms e.g. that'll, doesn't, can't
   - sentences starting with conjunctions. See the two examples above as well as many others.

9a. The writer suggests that a world dominated by advertising and sponsorship could be 'a nightmare'. Do you agree? Consider the writer's views as well as your own in your answer. *(20 marks)*

20 – 16 Answers will contain a majority of these points:
- well organised work that looks at a number of aspects and keeps close to the question e.g. Coronation Street's sponsorship benefits the programme makers but also provides entertainment for the audience and some cash prizes. It could also generate boredom, further intrusion by the advertisers and encouragement to eat an arguably unhealthy product
- the argument does not have to be balanced but there should be consideration from both angles
- points will be explained well and many will be backed up with examples
- reference will be made to points in the article such as manipulation of the product by the advertisers
- reference to the writer's attitude, she begins by calling it a 'tidal wave' of television sponsorship (a destructive metaphor) and ends with the word 'nightmare' and a sense of helplessness by the audience, 'utterly captive'
- expression is confident with few, if any, technical errors at the top end of this band.

15 – 11 Answers will contain a majority of these points:
- fair organisation although points may not have been presented in the best order
- there will be a need for more examples to support opinions
- some reference to the article but better use could have been made of key points
- good expression but vocabulary is more limited than top band work
- a more limited range of punctuation and some spellings errors.

10 – 6 Answers will contain a majority of these points:
- some organisation but points are likely to be presented as they occurred to the writer
- little development of ideas and few, if any, examples to support opinions
- little use of the article, a tendency for the essay to be opinionated
- fair but repetitive expression
- noticeable errors in punctuation and spelling.

5 or lower
- unorganised work with random ideas
- unoriginal thinking and opinionated views with no examples
- noticeable errors that may hamper the expression.

What's in an name?

Higher Level – Answers

9b. Crunchy Crisps have written to your school offering to pay for all the student exercise books if, in return, they can put an advert for their crisps on the back cover of each book. Write two letters; the first from Crunchy Crisps to your Headteacher proposing the deal and the advantages to the school, the second letter from the Headteacher accepting or declining the offer and saying why. *(20 marks)*

20 – 16 Answers will contain a majority of these points:
- *correct letter layouts, preferably with the sender's address*
- *clearly expressed opening paragraph that explains the context*
- *appropriate tone, polite, their arguments are made confidently*
- *the Crunchy Crisps letter justifies their approach with a number of benefits to the school, such as financial support for school equipment*
- *the letter from the Headteacher can accept or decline the offer but with clear reasons and refers to points made in their letter*
- *good structure to both letters*
- *technically excellent with few errors.*

15 – 11 Answers will contain a majority of these points:
- *correct letter layouts, preferably with the sender's address*
- *at least a sentence that sets the context for the letter*
- *a suitable tone for both letters but they will lack the subtlety and range of expression needed for the highest grade category*
- *the Crunchy Crisps letter justifies their approach with a few benefits to the school although these will not be as persuasive as the higher grade category – this may be due to the way it is expressed*
- *the letter from the Headteacher can accept or decline the offer but with good reasons*
- *good structure to both letters*
- *fair expression but some phrasing is repetitive technically good with a few errors in punctuation and spelling.*

10 – 6 Answers will contain a majority of these points:
- *correct letter layout*
- *the approach from the crisp company is likely to be clear but heavy handed, not building a persuasive argument*
- *the letter from the Headteacher might be brief*
- *one or both letters need better structure to make their points clearer*
- *expression is often repetitive*
- *technically fair but a number of noticeable errors.*

5 or lower
- *unorganised work with random ideas*
- *an unsuitable tone in one or both letters*
- *few good reasons for offering the sponsorship and accepting or declining it*
- *noticeable errors that may hamper the expression.*

9c. Sherry Ashworth's worst fears have been realised and the advertisers have taken control of Coronation Street or another soap opera of your choice. Write a few scenes in script form of this soap showing how the advertisers have muscled into the storylines. *(20 marks).*

20 – 16 Answers will contain a majority of these points:
- *a script layout which makes it clear who is speaking*
- *a lively mixture of dialogue totally suited to the soap opera style*
- *an eventful storyline with a variety of emerging plots even if they are barely developed*
- *plenty of product reference either in stage directions or dialogue, the scripts may be amusing*
- *technically excellent with few errors.*

15 – 11 Answers will contain a majority of these points:
- *a script layout which makes it clear who is speaking*
- *a good mixture of dialogue that adopts the soap opera style*
- *likely to be fewer storylines and less plot development, students may stick to one scene*
- *at least four product references, students may not see all the opportunities to advertise*
- *technically good with a few errors in punctuation and spelling.*

10 – 6 Answers will contain a majority of these points:
- *a script layout which usually makes it clear who is speaking*
- *dialogue is fair but the student has not picked up the nuances of the soaps, particularly short lines of dialogue and interruptions*
- *at least two product references, students have missed obvious opportunities to advertise*
- *technically fair but a number of noticeable errors.*

5 or lower
- *unorganised work, with random ideas*
- *the soap opera style has not been achieved*
- *product advertising is barely mentioned or so over done as to be totally unrealistic*
- *noticeable errors that may hamper the expression.*

Guide to grade boundaries		
45	– 42	A*
41	– 37	A
36	– 32	B
31	– 27	C
26	– 22	D
Below 22		U

All the rage

When you lose your rag on the road or have a tantrum at the checkout, it might prove to be the best thing you could do. CHRISTOPHER MIDDLETON on the pleasures and pitfalls of letting off steam

If there is one thing guaranteed to grab our attention, it is the sound of raised voices. In an age when most human drama is played out on television rather than in real life, the sight of someone losing their temper in public has acquired a kind of street-theatre status. Passers-by put down their shopping bags and stop to watch the action, and in no time at all, a sizable crowd will have gathered.

The fact is, anger is fascinating and, some would argue, good for us. A recent survey by National Opinion Poll (NOP) found that 90% of us flare up more often than we did a decade ago and that 10% admitted to losing their temper at least once a day. Three times that number had suffered from checkout rage, and being kept on hold on the telephone was voted even more stressful than road rage.

In another study, carried out by researchers in Belgium and reported in The Lancet medical journal, it was shown that patients suffering from heart disease who bottled up their feelings were four times more likely to die from a heart attack than those who gave vent to their spleen.

Maybe it is because there are so few opportunities to lose your temper publicly that it feels so good when you do. Once, there were shop assistants and other members of the service industries who were just plain rude, and with whom you were entirely justified in having a barney. These days, it's all: "I'm sorry you feel like that, sir. I'll contact customer services."

As a result, when someone does actually lose their temper, it tends to be quite spectacular, as if they are compensating for all those times they did not lose their rag in a smaller way. This could be the real reason behind all the rages that have become so fashionable: road rage, trolley rage, shopping rage and, my favourite, food rage. You would think we lived in a total rage age, but we do not. It is just that when it happens, we notice it more.

What is more, far from being in the grip of uncontrollable fury, we are surprisingly unspontaneous and calculating about who gets it in the neck when we do let rip. One unpleasant – but true – fact is that nine times out of 10, the person we pick on will be someone less equipped to defend themselves than we are.

"We tend to vent our anger upon people who aren't a threat," says Ben Williams, an Edinburgh-based corporate psychologist. "For example, if we are having problems at the office and the boss comes in and says, 'Working late?', we sigh and give him a watery smile. But if the office post boy comes in and says the same thing, he'll get an earbashing."

I am ashamed to say that I recognise those symptoms all too well. After a frustrating day at work, I like nothing better than to be rung up by someone I can bully with complete impunity. Best of all

All the rage

is the opening line "Who am I speaking to?", which gives me the chance to reply: "I'm not sure. Hold on, I'll just have a look." It is the perfect cue to be snide with them. Forgive me, please, man from the double glazing firm and woman from the kitchen design company whose representative just happens to be in my area. You may have suffered – but it made me feel much better.

There again, we should not kid ourselves that our veins run with mineral water rather than hot blood. According to Peter Collett, a behaviour expert at Oxford University: "We are by nature an aggressive nation, but the way we deal with it is to keep tight control on how we behave. We're afraid of the fracas we might cause if we ever really let ourselves go."

Mind you, there are plenty of people who relish being angry all the time; people who get a kick out of their permanent bear-with-a-sore-head label. These are the dreaded stress-carriers – they dish it out to everyone else in generous portions, but do not themselves get all churned up in the process.

Sifting through my own past, I find it hard to pick out a single occasion where I can honestly claim to have been in the grip of pure, righteous anger, unsullied by any secondary considerations. I know, when I was 10, my real reason for punching Stephen Page on the jaw was entirely suspect. His only offence was to utter the word "stupid" when my mother asked him not to stand on our flowerbeds.

"I didn't mean she was stupid, I meant I was stupid to be standing there," he wailed, picking himself up from the ground. And I'm sure he was telling the truth. I also know that in my heart of hearts, the reason for my loss of temper was that he had always irritated me and this was the perfect excuse to punch him.

"In order for anger not to destroy trust between relatives or colleagues, it must be directed solely at the person's behaviour not at the person themselves," advises Williams. "Anger should be used like a samurai sword: quickly, honourably and accurately."

Oh dear. You mean that when my wife messes up the map-reading (again) and I immediately jump from complaining about that to moaning about the way she never puts the lid back on the Marmite jar, I am acting, in some way, dishonourably or trying to score cheap points?

You mean that I was somehow in the wrong when I ruined an entire dinner party by storming out because the hostess kept talking over me? You think I should have sworn less loudly and done less door slamming? You think that because I did not want to go to the party in the first place, and did not really want to continue the friendship anyway, I was motivated by anything other than pure moral outrage? Well, you are probably right.

As final proof that anger is truly man made and something we can control if we choose, consider the tale of this run-in which could have erupted into a huge scene if I had not known what the lawyers call "the other party".

I turned a corner in the car and almost ran straight into an oncoming Volvo. We both braked, and almost before the cars had screeched to a halt, leapt out, furious and ready to commit any number of road-rage atrocities.

Suddenly, I realised that this idiot was my next-door neighbour. Somehow the fuel just drained straight out of our anger tanks. We laugh about it now, but had we been strangers and started on each other with spanners, we could both now be doing five years in Pentonville.

© Christopher Middleton /
The Sunday Times, 1997.
(Photocopying allowed for classroom use only)

Higher Level – Questions

All the rage

Time: _____

Read 'All the Rage' then answer the questions.

1. From the first paragraph, what reason does the writer suggest for people being so interested in watching real arguments?
   (2 marks)

2. From the second paragraph mention one fact from the author and one opinion.
   (2 marks)

3. From a medical point of view, can it be better to lose your temper? Justify your opinion with a fact from the article.
   (2 marks)

4. Does the author view most rages as real or as a pretence? Give two examples from the article explaining your view.
   (4 marks)

5. Explain what the author means when he says, 'we should not kid ourselves that our veins run with mineral water rather than hot blood'.
   (2 marks)

6. Mention two examples from the article; one where the author was embarrassed that he lost his temper and one where he feels pleased that he did.
   (4 marks)

7. What does the writer see as being the ultimate danger of losing your temper?
   (2 marks)

Choose one of the following questions:

8a. Imagine that 'School Rage' exists; this is where students can become out of control because of their anger. Write an advice leaflet for younger teachers on ways they might identify School Rage before anything major occurs and what they might do if a student displays School Rage.
   (20 marks)

   or

8b. Should we learn never to lose our temper or become violent? Would this produce a better world? Using the article and your own knowledge write an essay that considers these questions.
   (20 marks)

   or

8c. A student in Year 10 in your school has had a fight with another in the class. One of the students had to be taken to hospital because of suspected concussion, the other student claims to have been taunted relentlessly and to have just 'snapped' and hit out. Imagine you are the Head of Year and have to give an assembly on the problems and dangers of fighting and the need for cooperation, using this incident as your starting point. Write the assembly speech that will be given to Years 10 and 11.   *(20 marks)*

All the rage

All the rage Marking Suggestions

Advised Time: 75 minutes

1. From the first paragraph, what reason does the writer suggest for people being so interested in watching real arguments? *(2 marks)*
   - it is a rare sight, particularly to see it live as opposed to on television.

2. From the second paragraph mention one fact from the author and one opinion. *(2 marks)*
   (Opinion) In the first line, anger is fascinating and, some would argue, good for us. This is an opinion although he begins by saying 'the fact is'
   (Fact) Any one of the following:
   - NOP found 90% flare up more often than a decade ago
   - 10% admit to losing their temper once a day
   - three times that number had suffered from checkout rage
   - telephone rage was even more stressful than road rage.

3. From a medical point of view, can it be better to lose your temper? Justify your opinion with a fact from the article. *(2 marks)*
   - in the third paragraph it was shown that bottling up feelings can be harmful for heart disease patients
   - evidence for this has been carried out by researchers in Belgium and it was reported in The Lancet medical journal.

4. Does the author view most rages as real or as a pretence? Give two examples from the article explaining your view. *(4 marks)*
   - no, the author consistently makes the argument that rages are controlled 'I find it hard to pick out a single occasion where I can honestly claim to have been in the grip of pure, righteous anger, unsullied by any secondary considerations.'
   One mark for each of these examples up to two:
   - we tend to pick on people who aren't a threat, e.g. the office boy
   - we have prepared sarcastic answers for uninvited telephone callers
   - he once punched a boy because it was the perfect excuse
   - he stormed out of a dinner party because he didn't want to be there anyway and didn't like the people
   - he controlled his anger when he nearly drove into his neighbour's car.

5. Explain what the author means when he says, we should not kid ourselves that our veins run with mineral water rather than hot blood. *(2 marks)*
   Two marks for a clear explanation:
   - we should not fool ourselves that we are passive, gentle people. We are motivated by feelings.

6. Mention two examples from the article; one where the author was embarrassed that he lost his temper and one where he feels pleased that he did. *(4 marks)*
   Two marks for each up to a maximum of four:
   - (Embarrassed) Criticising his wife, scoring cheap points
   - (Embarrassed) Storming out of the dinner party
   - (Embarrassed) Nearly hitting his neighbour over the car incident
   - (Pleased) Hitting Stephen Page for saying "stupid"
   - (Pleased) Insulting telephone callers at the end of a frustrating day at work even though he begins by saying 'I am ashamed'.

7. What does the writer see as being the ultimate danger of losing your temper? *(2 marks)*
   - seriously injuring a person
   - ending up in prison for doing this.

8a. Imagine that 'School Rage' exists; this is where students can become out of control because of their anger. Write an advice leaflet for younger teachers on ways they might identify School Rage before anything major occurs and what they might do if a student displays School Rage. *(20 marks)*

20 - 16 Answers will contain a majority of these points:
- a leaflet style to the piece; features such as sections for each topic, topics indicated by title, a layout that is helpful and not muddled or confusing. Illustrations or diagrams can be commended but are not essential and may disadvantage the student if too much time has been taken on them
- a friendly tone to the piece, reassuring – at this level markers should not worry if the tone is slightly patronising
- good ideas for identifying school rage such as rises in class noise, where students sit, lack of attention to the teacher or the work
- good ideas for handling School Rage such as getting the disrupter out of the classroom, sending for help from a senior member of staff
- the piece is well-organised and substantial in length
- technically excellent with confident use of punctuation and few spelling errors.

15 - 11 Answers will contain a majority of these points:
- a leaflet style to the piece; features such as sections for each topic, topics indicated by title, there has been some attempt at a layout although it probably suggests that more thought or planning would have made it better. Illustrations or diagrams can be commended but are not essential and may disadvantage the student if too much time has been taken on them
- the tone is friendly but it is likely to be factual and demanding, lacking the subtlety needed for the higher grades
- some good ideas for identifying problems, at least three properly explained
- some suitable ideas for handling School Rage, the ideas are appropriate for a teacher to use
- the piece is organised although time may not have been used well to make sure each part of the leaflet is completed well
- technically good with a varied vocabulary, there may be a few errors in spelling and punctuation

Higher Level – Answers

All the rage

10 - 6 Answers will contain a majority of these points:
- *an attempt at a leaflet with sections and titles*
- *the piece needs better organisation*
- *they have satisfied the brief but the tone is blunt and factual or too colloquial*
- *there are some ideas for identifying School Rage, at least two*
- *at least two solutions for solving School Rage although the ideas may not be very sophisticated or tactful*
- *expression is repetitive at the lower end and a noticeable number of technical errors.*

5 or under Answers will contain at least one of these features:
- *a misunderstanding of the task*
- *short, shallow ideas with no planning*
- *many technical errors, at least one on each line*

8b. Should we learn never to lose our temper or become violent? Would this produce a better world? Using the article and your own knowledge write an essay that considers these questions. *(20 marks)*

20 - 16 Answers will contain a majority of these points:
- *a good structure to the piece with evidence of planning*
- *views presented in a logical order, i.e. a clear line of argument*
- *views supported by examples, some may be taken from the article*
- *mature confident expression with a varied vocabulary*
- *technically excellent with few errors.*

15-11 Answers will contain a majority of these points:
- *some planning and structure to the piece*
- *a varied range of views although the discussion may dwell too much on one half of the question*
- *some views supported by examples, preferably at least one from the article*
- *varied expression although the tone may be repetitive in places*
- *technically good at the top end of this band but more frequent errors at the lower end.*

10 - 6 Answers will contain a majority of these points:
- *some planning to the piece if only evident by new paragraphs for each idea*
- *points are likely to be unconnected so there is no line of argument*
- *general points, a majority will not be supported by examples or a point oversupported by a long and probably tedious example*
- *expression is repetitive at the lower end with a significant number of errors in punctuation and spelling.*

5 or below Answers will contain at least one of these features:
- *a misunderstanding of the task*
- *short, shallow ideas with no planning*
- *many technical errors, at least one on each line*

8c. A student in Year 10 in your school has had a fight with another in the class. One of the students had to be taken to hospital because of suspected concussion, the other student claims to have been taunted relentlessly and to have just 'snapped' and hit out. Imagine you are the Head of Year and have to give an assembly on the problems and dangers of fighting and the need for cooperation, using this incident as your starting point. Write the assembly speech that will be given to Years 10 and 11. *(20 marks)*

20-16 Answers will contain a majority of these points:
- *a good structure to the piece with evidence of planning*
- *a suitable introduction that sets the context*
- *points presented in a logical order, i.e. a clear line of argument*
- *reference made to the incident (as requested) but used as a springboard for a wider discussion*
- *a balance covering both points requested in the question*
- *mature confident expression with a varied vocabulary*
- *an awareness of the audience, language will not be too pompous or condescending*
- *the very best pieces will make good use of speech techniques such as deliberate repetition, rhetorical questions and impact at strategic parts of the talk*
- *technically excellent with few errors.*

15 - 11 Answers will contain a majority of these points:
- *some planning and structure to the piece*
- *some form of introduction that at least explains the topic of the assembly*
- *a more limited range of points, the speech is likely to keep closely to the brief without seeing the opportunities for a wider and more interesting talk*
- *little if any use of speech techniques although there should be an awareness of the audience being addressed*
- *varied expression although the tone may be repetitive in places*
- *technically good at the top end of this band but more frequent errors at the lower end.*

10 - 6 Answers will contain a majority of these points:
- *some planning to the piece if only evident by new paragraphs for each idea*
- *the talk is likely to have covered the main points requested in a very short space and then just repeats what was already said*
- *at the lower end the piece reads more like an essay with little awareness of the audience*
- *expression is repetitive at the lower end with a significant number of errors in punctuation and spelling.*

5 or below Answers will contain at least one of these features:
- *a misunderstanding of the task*
- *short, shallow ideas with no planning*
- *many technical errors, at least one on each line*

A guide to grade boundaries	
38 - 36	A*
35 - 32	A
31 - 28	B
27 - 24	C
23 - 20	D
Below 20	U

The National Lottery - who wins? who loses?

Most people in the UK enjoy a flutter on the National Lottery, but our survey raises serious concerns about how it's being run and where the money raised is going.

WHICH? SAYS

The National Lottery is enjoyed by millions and is clearly a successful way of raising money for good causes. But we think there is a serious conflict of interest in the role of the Lottery regulator, Oflot. It should no longer be responsible for maximising the proceeds from the Lottery but instead concentrate on safeguarding players' interests and regulating the operator, Camelot.

A clear national strategy is also needed to ensure that the billions of pounds of public money being raised are distributed fairly and benefit the whole community.

There's no doubt that the National Lottery raises huge sums of money. Since it began in November 1994, we've spent around £9.5 billion on tickets and scratch cards.

When the Lottery was launched, the Government promised benefits for all, and it set up the Office of the National Lottery (Oflot) to make sure that the Lottery was properly run. Two years on, what do people think about the way the Lottery is being run and how their money is being spent? To find out, we spoke to more than 2,000 people around England, Scotland and Wales.

Who plays?

The vast majority of people have played the Lottery at least once, but there are big differences between the types of people who play the weekly draw and those who buy scratch cards.

Oflot says that, contrary to many people's concerns, those who are least well-off aren't spending more on the Lottery than other groups. However, our survey clearly shows that, while this is true generally, it is not the case with scratch cards.

Three-quarters of the people we spoke to had played the weekly draw; those in full-time employment were most likely to play. With scratch cards, however, the pattern is very different. Overall, 38 per cent of people had bought scratch cards. But looking more closely at the figures, 55 per cent of unemployed people and 56 per cent of 15- to 24-year olds had bought scratch cards.

Child's play

It is illegal to sell Lottery tickets and scratch cards to anyone under 16. Under the National Lottery Act, the Director General of Oflot must authorise only the promotion of lotteries which have sufficient controls to prevent people under 16 years old from playing.

In our survey, more than two-thirds of people said it bothered them that under 16-year-olds played the Lottery. The same proportion felt that a lot more should be done to prevent this. Most people also felt the age limit should be raised to 18.

For well over a year, there has been evidence – some of it from Oflot's own surveys - that many children under 16 could be playing the Lottery. Yet it was only last month that Oflot acted to stop under age playing. Oflot has said that retailers will have to display 'explicit warnings' about under-age sales, as well as a phone number that people can call if they see tickets being sold to children under 16.

These changes have not only come late in the day, but are a soft option - Oflot has powers to force Camelot to take more responsibility for the problem. This is because each new scratch card game requires a new licence from Oflot, so it is perfectly possible for it to refuse to allow any new games to be launched until Camelot deals with the sale of tickets to children.

Playing by the rules

One of the reasons that Oflot took so long to deal with under-age playing could be the conflicting aspects of its role. When the Government set up Oflot, it gave the Director General three main tasks. First, he had to appoint a company to operate the Lottery. After this, he must ensure that the Lottery is run properly and that players' interests are protected. Finally, as long as these have been done, he must also ensure that as much money as possible is raised for good causes.

But Oflot seems unclear about which role is most important. In its latest annual report, the Director General makes several references to having achieved a 'balance' between these duties. However, his job is not to strike a balance, but to put the regulation of the operator and the interests of the players first.

Other evidence suggests that the interests of the players are not always his first priority. Last year, the Director General warned MPs on the Public Accounts Committee against publishing their concerns about G Tech, one of Camelot's major shareholders, as he felt this could have 'adverse impact' on Lottery revenue.

The need to maximise proceeds was also the reason he gave to the National Audit Office to explain why he hadn't carried out certain checks on the integrity and security of Camelot's computer systems – despite the fact that security was described as 'of paramount importance' in the National Lottery's vision statement.

Where does all the money go?

The National Lottery was set up to raise money for the Arts and Sports Councils, the Charities Board, the National Heritage Memorial Fund and the Millennium Commission.

The Government left it to these bodies to decide where the money is spent. However, it promised that this money

The National Lottery

would be additional to existing government expenditure in these areas, and provide benefits for all, regardless of income.

When we asked people what they thought about how the money was being distributed, around three quarters said that too much money went on a few big projects. The same number thought the money should be distributed equally to all regions of the country.

Regional differences

We also asked people if they thought money spent on the Lottery in their area should go back to good causes in their area, and found strong regional differences. Around 60 per cent of people in the North and the Midlands agreed. Only 35 per cent of those in London did.

Indeed, a far greater proportion of the Lottery proceeds has gone to London than players there spend – a fact that seems to be reflected in our findings.

Some of the reasons for these regional differences may well lie in the conditions attached to grants by most of the funding bodies.

For example, to get a Lottery grant, most applicants must be able to find other money for anything from 10 to 50 per cent of the total cost of a project. Local authorities are one of the main sources of such funding. However, the amount of money they have available for this varies enormously – and some have none at all.

Grants are generally available only for capital projects – museums and sports facilities, for example. Applicants must show that they will be able to pay to maintain and run these. Some areas are more likely to be given grants than others because these costs may have to be met by charging high entrance fees – an option most likely to be possible in better-off areas or areas which attract lots of tourists.

Clearly, the money the Lottery raises has great potential. But if it is truly to benefit everyone, it should not be subject to the vagaries of the various distribution bodies.

OUR SURVEY

Last September, we interviewed 2,029 adults aged 15 and over throughout England, Scotland and Wales, asking them about their experiences of the National Lottery and their attitudes to it.

Which? January 1997
Published by the Consumers' Association

WHO WANTS TO BE A MILLIONAIRE?

If you want to get rich quick, buying a Lottery ticket is probably not the best way. But, according to our survey, most people have no idea of their chances of winning.

Only about a fifth of people knew that the odds against them winning the jackpot are almost 14 million to one. Almost half said they had no idea; the rest were evenly split between those who overestimated their chances and those who underestimated them.

To be fair, 60 per cent of the players in our survey said they played for fun and weren't worried about the chances of winning (though people who played every week were less likely to feel this way than those who played occasionally).

However, two-thirds thought there shouldn't be such large jackpots and more than four out of five felt there should be more smaller prizes.

It is difficult to compare the likelihood of winning the Lottery draw with other forms of gambling because, unlike horse racing or the Pools say, draws are random and skill or knowledge of the game cannot improve the odds. However, one bookmaker told us that the only odds he gives that are longer than those on winning the Lottery jackpot are those against Screaming Lord Sutch becoming the next prime minister – currently offered at 15 million to one.

Higher Level – Questions

The National Lottery

Time: _____

Read the article about the National Lottery and then answer all of the questions that follow.

1. What chance does a person have of winning the lottery jackpot?
   (2 marks)

2. From the opening column, 'There's no doubt…', give three facts about the lottery.
   (3 marks)

3. In your own words explain why the south of England appears to be getting more lottery grants.
   (4 marks)

4. From this article, what are the main concerns about the lottery?
   (5 marks)

5. Your school wishes to apply for a lottery grant to improve its performing arts **or** sports facilities. Write a letter of application to the Lottery Board for a grant explaining what you want funding for and how it will benefit the school.
   (16 marks)

The National Lottery

The National Lottery Marking Suggestions

Advised Time: 60 minutes

1. What chance does a person have of winning the lottery jackpot? *(2 marks)*
   Almost 14 million to 1.

2. From the opening column, 'There's no doubt…', give three facts about the lottery. *(3 marks)*
   - it began in November 1994
   - 9.5 Billion has been spent so far
   - Oflot was set up to regulate the lottery.

3. In your own words explain why the south of England appears to be getting more lottery grants. *(4 marks)*
   Note: Most of these points are inter-related and answers that indicate this should be rewarded.
   - to get a grant, applicants must put in 10 - 50% of the total project cost
   - local authorities should contribute but often cannot
   - some institutions will need to charge higher price entrance tickets
   - the south is likely to have better off areas and tourist areas such as London.

4. From this article, what are the main concerns about the lottery? *(5 marks)*
   - unemployed and a substantial number of young people are buying scratch cards
   - children under 16 are gambling
   - Oflot should protect players' interests more, there is a conflict of interests
   - security could be tighter
   - Lottery funds may not be distributed fairly around the country.

5. Your school wishes to apply for a lottery grant to improve its performing arts or sports facilities. Write a letter of application to the Lottery Board for a grant explaining what you want funding for and how it will benefit the school.

   16 – 13 Answers will contain a majority of these points:
   - correct letter layout (suitable address such as the school, correct salutation and conclusion)
   - well-organised work with each idea or point paragraphed
   - the letter could outline the current situation of the school before outlining its proposals
   - students will have noted the terms and conditions mentioned in the article (last column) and should refer to support from other sources as well
   - proposals are likely to be well-supported with relevant and sensible reasons, for example, the facilities might benefit the community both in use and in keeping young people interested during and after school
   - wide vocabulary is used and the tone of the letter is confident and polite
   - technically, the work is almost faultless at the top end of this mark.

   12 – 9 Answers will contain a majority of these points:
   - correct letter layout (suitable address such as the school, correct salutation and conclusion)
   - an organised approach
   - proposals will be supported with reasons but they may be superficial and not clearly explain how it will benefit the school
   - the tone is more abrupt and demanding caused by a more limited range of expression
   - technically good at the top end of this mark.

   8 – 4 Answers will contain a majority of these points:
   - some attempt at a letter layout
   - the request is likely to lead straight into the need for funding in an unsubtle way
   - justification will be superficial with the request not thought through
   - work will jump from point to point and may repeat itself
   - technically the work is fair but unchecked and casual errors should place it near the bottom of this category.

   Advice: There is room for teacher discretion here. Students who make applications for grants for sporting facilities <u>and</u> performing arts should gain the lowest marks as this is not what is requested. However, you may feel that this is too harsh a lesson for students who are inexperienced or who write well but inappropriately to the question. Work not presented in letter format should also receive very low marks.

Guide to Grade Boundaries		
30 – 28	A*
27 – 25	A
24 – 21	B
20 – 17	C
16 – 13	D
Below 13	U

Sharing not Buying

In this issue, US green design guru Victor Papanek explains his ten questions to ask before shopping

The easiest way to save resources and energy and to cut down on waste is to use less. This statement is so simple as to sound banal, yet it can serve as a guide to action. Also implied is the idea of consuming less, buying less, making do with what we have already – even at times ridding ourselves of all the unnecessary gadgets and duplicates that so hideously clutter up our lives. All this is just plain common sense, yet it is an approach to living that seems to be fairly rare at the moment.

1. Do I really need it?

Before making a purchasing decision, the first – yet frequently unasked – question should be: do I really need it? Have I been persuaded to buy it because it offers some real advantages over what I use now, or because it will actually help me in my learning, working, leisure? Will it in some way bring greater enchantment to my life and those dear to me? Or will it – under the guise of offering greater convenience – make living more complicated or become a placebo for the stresses we all experience? Yet even if we can honestly say that we do need the object, and are sure that we are not buying it in the forlorn hope that it will make us more powerful, wiser, or more attractive, nor prompted by some temporary whim or the seductive whisperings of the advertisers, we face many further decisions.

- *Will something else serve the same purpose, possibly something I already own?*
- *Can I use a different method to accomplish the same task?*
- *Do I understand the device, or do I have a friend who can explain the advantages or disadvantages?*
- *Is it well made and made to last?*
- *Can faults be readily diagnosed?*
- *Can it be repaired and will spare parts be available?*
- *Does it have extra features that may be unnecessary, yet add to the number of things that could go wrong?*
- *Could it atrophy some of my skills?*

When these questions have been answered, we are ready to turn to a whole new area of considerations.

2. Can I buy it secondhand?

As a working product designer I must point out that the producers *really* 'don't make things the way they used to any more'. There are shops run by charity organisations in most large towns. Frequently many of the things they sell are in fact brand new. In many towns in the United States, for example, graduating students, leaving their flats and houses for good at the end of the academic year, frequently abandon new clothing, small appliances, furniture and books. At one university after the students had left, building services found more than a thousand shirts, scores of dresses and suits, as well as enough cosmetics to satisfy a small town, all still in the original wrappings.

3. Can I buy it at a discount?

There may be an item that you really do have to buy and where a fairly new technology is involved. If the technology is electronic and therefore difficult to examine for malfunctions – a CD-player, for instance – then it is always possible to buy a leftover of the previous year or a discontinued model through a discount shop. Many technical devices can also be obtained factory-reconditioned from dealers, often with a warranty. These are the high-tech equivalents of 'factory seconds' of crockery, cookware or cutlery that bear faint imperfections in finish or colour, or discontinued or overstocked styles. These and so-called 'remaindered' books can all usually be bought at shops that specialize in such goods.

4. Can I borrow it?

If the object you need will only be used infrequently, or just once or twice, can it be borrowed? Personal experience has shown me that most people are only too pleased to be asked to help share their expertise and some specialised tool or apparatus that they own. Most of my neighbours in Lawrence have furnished their basements with a lavish collection of small electric drills, orbital sanders, circular saws, shapers and band saws, as well as an abundance of hand tools. Most of these tools are only needed for small repairs around the house, and their proud owners are happy to lend them out and see them used.

5. Can I rent it?

Renting is one step further from outright ownership. We routinely rent certain things when buying them would pose inconveniences quite apart from the cash spent on them. On a business trip we rent a car at the airport to get to our final destination. We use the local library to catch up on our reading and listening. Whilst on holiday we frequently rent a video camera, or a moped or a bicycle to get around, or a tent, beach umbrella and deckchairs. In most towns there are shops devoted to hiring out equipment for working on the car, building a garage or sundeck, or for gardening. Some places specialize in renting out furniture and major electrical appliances to students or other temporary residents; some shops rent drinking glasses, cutlery and table settings for parties and receptions.

6. Can I lease it?

Leasing is essentially a long-term rental contract. In many countries telephones are leased rather than owned – maintenance, repair, insurance and replacement are then no longer the individual's concern. Cars are leased by companies and, increasingly, by individual owners who recognize that in the real world they never really own their car at all since they tend to trade it in for a new model just after – or slightly before – making the last of their payments. With the ever more rapid technological changes in personal computers, and the obsolescence of entire hardware systems within years rather than decades, it is obvious that leasing a home-computer is a better idea than buying.

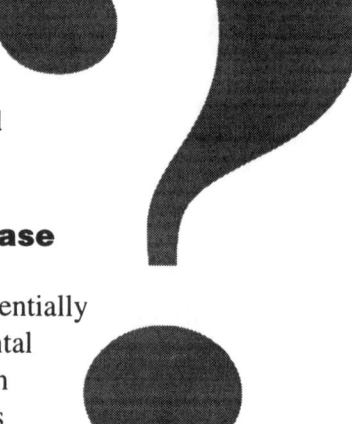

7. Can I share it?

Assume the existence of a neighbourhood or community centre. Here one could share items that could be communally owned. There might be sewing machines; computers and computer printers; a large area of wall-mounted lockers, each of which is one household's bulk frozen-food storage. There could also be workshop and gardening tools – possibly even a small crafts workshop – and it might also be feasible to share cameras, camcorders, slide projectors and even bicycles, shopping carts and some types of sports equipment. Such a 'Sharing Library' could also stock goods that folk in the neighbourhood have discarded as no longer suited to their needs, or left behind when moving away – a sort of revival of the 'free stores' of the hippies in the late 1960s. There is no question that this place would also serve as the local recycling centre.

8. Can we own it as a group?

Sharing to cut down on waste, to make things more affordable or just to reduce the amount of raw materials locked up in goods can operate on many different levels. I was favourably impressed to notice that in Denmark, designers and architects often share subscriptions to expensive international professional magazines. A copy of, say, *Domus* or *Bau-Biologie* will have a list of ten or twelve participating members of the reading circle clipped to it, and it is forwarded in turn to each on the list, finally ending up in the local library for the public at large. Clearly this not only reduces subscription costs for each individual by nine-tenths or more, but – which is even more important – it cuts down on the wastefulness of paper and printing inks as well as transport. Many people in the Scandinavian countries subscribe to ordinary consumer magazines in the same way. It is obvious that this example could serve as a template for sharing in many other fields.

9. Can I build it myself?

The so-called average person, anywhere in the world, is better informed and more aware of his or her needs than any designer or architect. It is therefore plain that the design needs of most people can best be served by the users themselves working in close collaboration with a designer. The next step is to suggest that people should be empowered to design their own solutions to their own specific requirements. These observations are not in anyway startlingly new, but draw on precedent. Vernacular architecture is not only usually self-built, but also self-designed. Throughout many centuries end-users would work directly with a local builder or craftsman to add rooms to a house, have a desk made, build a carriage or have a cool-space dug for food storage. Yet these remarks are not intended to suggest a regression towards a Luddite attack on the machine age and our Post-Modern existence. The emphasis is rather that the close relationship between using and making, being and becoming, needs to be strengthened once again. Even today large groups take pleasure in re-inventing, changing, modifying and building their own tools and environments.

10. Can I buy a kit?

With this in mind, I would like to turn to an additional group of options. On the most basic level, we are all becoming used to the fact that many of the goods we buy now come to us in somewhat unfinished form. Mail order catalogues frequently carry the phrase, 'Some self-assembly required' in small print at the bottom of the page. We realize that the wine-rack or bookshelf we buy will be delivered as a flat package. The bicycle we buy for our child, even the pram for the baby, will not arrive ready for use. The reason for making the users into – frequently unwilling – participants in completing the construction lies in the saving the manufacturer makes in shipping charges. Generally the costs reflect bulk more than weight. This new assumption on the part of manufacturers, that people will finish the assembly of a product themselves, has beneficial side-effects. When building things from a kit, there is a good learning experience for the customer. It becomes simpler to understand how and why the gadget works. More importantly to my mind, the design of objects that must be completed by the customer is beginning to influence how goods look. If self-assembly were to be combined with Design for Disassembly, the aesthetic results would be radical and fresh.

This extract is reproduced with permission from The Green Imperative by Victor Papanek (Thames & Hudson 1995) ISBN 0 500 27846 6. It is available in paperback and costs £14.95 from: Thames & Hudson, 30 Bloomsbury Street, London WC1B 3QP.

Sharing not buying
Higher Level – Questions

Time: _____

Read the article "Sharing Not Buying". Answer the questions.

1. Look at the section, Can I buy it secondhand? Give three generalisations the writer makes in this section.
   (3 marks)

2. What methods does the writer use to make his views persuasive to an audience? You should think about how he puts over his ideas rather than the ideas themselves.
   (7 marks)

3. What problems can you see in trying to convince people to adopt the writer's ideas? Refer closely to the article in your answer.
   (8 marks)

Answer one question below.

4a. Taking some of the writer's ideas and adding your own, write an article for students in your year that might persuade them to change their shopping habits.
   (25 marks)

   or

4b. Look again at the section, Can I share it? You have been asked to set up a Sharing Library in your street. Write a letter to your neighbours outlining the scheme, its advantages and how the scheme might get started.
   (25 marks)

   or

4c. The Association of Department Store Retailers has been asked to respond to Victor Papanek's article. Write their article which will be published in a popular magazine read by a wide age range. The title and theme is, Why We Need To Buy New Items.
   (25 marks)

Sharing not buying Marking Suggestions

Advised Time: 75 minutes

1. Look at the section, Can I buy it secondhand? Give three generalisations the writer makes in this section. *(3 marks)*
   (Any three of the four below)
   - producers don't make things the way they used to any more
   - charity shops frequently sell brand new items
   - there are charity shops in most large towns
   - graduating students frequently abandon new items

2. How does the writer make his views persuasive to an audience? You should think about how he puts over his ideas rather than the ideas themselves.
   (7 marks maximum - one for each point explained well and a further mark if an example is used.) Half mark for a poorly explained point. Well-explained points other than those below can receive a mark.
   - short sentences enable easier understanding
   - simple expression, avoidance of technical terms
   - question and answer approach
   - use of bullet points that 'tests' the reader's attitude
   - frequent examples and anecdotes to support ideas
   - tone/style is a direct 'talkative' approach to the reader
   - original and interesting ideas based on the actual behaviour of consumers.

3. What problems can you see in trying to convince people to adopt the writer's ideas? Refer closely to the article in your answer.
   (8 marks maximum - some ideas are suggested below but a well-explained point, supported by a quotation earns two marks.)
   - people's habits and attitudes can be hard to change, most people enjoy shopping
   - people may not be able to choose exactly what they want, especially with shared items
   - the advertisers and producers will object to their products not being purchased
   - people may be possessive
   - it may be more convenient to own the item, particularly if it is used frequently, rather than borrow it
   - people might exploit renting and leasing costs
   - loaned items might become damaged or lost or may not be loaned for fear of this
   - shared or loaned items might wear out quicker through frequent use
   - some people may not enjoy or want to assemble their goods from a kit
   - some people may not live in close communities (distance as well as attitude) where it is easy to contact and share with neighbours.

4a. Taking some of the writer's ideas and some of your own, write an article for students in your year that might persuade them to change their shopping habits.

   25 – 20 Answers will contain a majority of these points:
   - suitable tone for teenagers, persuasive, possibly using the question and answer technique from the original article
   - a careful choice of ideas from the article but in their own words
   - well structured
   - useful and relevant examples to support ideas e.g. the advantages of sharing if you have a low income, how items are often abandoned when people move
   - as the piece is for teenagers, informal and slang terms are acceptable and desirable if it helps in the persuasive tone
   - technically excellent with confident use of vocabulary and punctuation and few spelling errors.

   19 - 14 Answers will contain a majority of these points:
   - a suitable tone for the audience, still a sense that it 'speaks' to the reader
   - some examples to support ideas
   - some ideas drawn from the original article, those close to the original wording get lower marks in this category
   - some structure to the piece but points may not be presented in the best order
   - a varied vocabulary
   - technically good.

   13 – 8 Answers will contain a majority of these points:
   - the piece might seem more like an essay for a teacher than an article for students
   - good ideas mentioned but possibly repeated or overexplained
   - the persuasive tone might not be subtle and therefore not persuasive!
   - some structure to the piece but the ideas are not in the best order
   - the piece is underdeveloped probably due to bad time management
   - a pedestrian vocabulary
   - some punctuation might be misplaced and spelling is noticeable as a problem.

   7 or below Answers will contain a majority of these points:
   - a misunderstanding of the task
   - wrong tone
   - poor expression
   - few to no examples
   - no discernible structure
   - technically weak with frequent errors
   - marks at this level would fail the student in this section.

4b. Look again at the section, Can I share it? You have been asked to set up a Sharing Library in your street. Write a letter to your neighbours outlining the scheme, its advantages and how the scheme might get started.

   25 – 20 Answers will contain a majority of these points:
   - letter has the correct layout and preferably a contact address
   - letter is well structured and introduces the scheme
   - possibly use of bullet points to show the scheme's advantages
   - tone of letter is suitable for an adult reading audience

Sharing not buying
Higher Level – Answers

- letter is not too ambitious, it is meant to outline the scheme
- how the scheme is to be started is clearly explained e.g. what items could be exhanged, how long for, whether deposits are required
- technically excellent with confident use of punctuation and few spelling errors.

19 – 14 Answers will contain a majority of these points:
- letter has the correct layout and possibly a contact address
- letter is structured and explains the scheme
- the tone is less confident than top band work, likely to be a more limited vocabulary
- there will be reference to how the scheme will start, for example the date of a meeting
- technically good, few errors in punctuation and common words.

13 – 8 Answers will contain a majority of these points:
- letter should still have the correct layout but may lack a contact address
- scheme may be explained in simple language and may not be persuasive
- some structure to the piece but the ideas are not in the best order
- the piece is likely to be underdeveloped due to bad time management
- there should still be reference to how the scheme will start
- some punctuation might be misplaced and spelling is noticeable as a problem.

7 or below Answers will contain a majority of these points:
- a misunderstanding of the task
- wrong tone for a neighbourhood audience
- poor expression
- not in letter format
- no reference to how the scheme will start
- poor structure
- technically weak
- marks at this level would fail the student in this section.

4c. The Association of Department Store Retailers has been asked to respond to Victor Papanek's article. Write their article that will be published in a popular magazine read by a wide age range. The title and theme is, Why We Need To Buy New Items.

25 – 20 Answers will contain a majority of these points:
- article format, for example, use of headline and subheaders
- close reference to the original article and well-justified counter arguments such as the effect on industries, shops and employment
- awareness of the 'wide audience'
- an appealing tone and use of relevant and familiar examples
- technically excellent with confident use of punctuation and few spelling errors.

19 – 14 Answers will contain a majority of these points:
- article format
- reference to the original article although the counter arguments might be too general or less confident
- good ideas and the writer keeps close to the title set
- good structure
- awareness of the audience but possibly not the skill to involve a wide age range throughout the piece
- technically good, few errors in spelling and punctuation.

13 – 8 Answers will contain a majority of these points:
- the piece might seem more like an essay for a teacher than an article for a wide age range
- some ideas mentioned but explained poorly or not in a good order
- possibly no reference to the original article
- the piece is likely to be underdeveloped
- a pedestrian vocabulary
- some punctuation might be misplaced and spelling is noticeable as a problem.

7 or below Answers will contain a majority of these points:
- a misunderstanding of the task
- wrong tone for an article and for the audience
- unconvincing arguments by the retailers
- technically weak
- marks at this level would fail the student in this section.

Guide to grade boundaries:		
43	– 39	A*
38	– 34	A
33	– 29	B
28	– 24	C
23	– 19	D
Below 19		U

A Journey along the SILK ROUTE

**From Kashgar to the Gates of Peking by Special Train
14 days fully inclusive from £1995.00**

Crossing and visiting mighty rivers, oases, great deserts, bazaars and the hidden treasures of the Silk Road visiting Bishket, Lake Issyk Kul, Naryn, Kashgar, Turfan and the Flaming Mountains, Dunhuang, Jiayuguan, and the end of the Great Wall of China, Xian and the Terracotta Army, Luoyang and Peking

For one time only during 1997 we shall be operating a special train along the Silk Road from Peking to Urumchi, thus enabling the traveller a programme of visits that otherwise would be difficult to accomplish. Any alternative way would certainly be less comfortable and more expensive. In being off the normal, well-trodden tourist track, this area of China has remained remote and, to a large extent, unspoilt. It introduces the traveller to a China of many different minority races, religions, ways of life, and through the progression of the journey the changing features of the people bring home the fact that China is not solely comprised of Han Chinese.

During the 1950s Mao and Khrushchev had a vision of throwing a railway line across the vast wastes of the Taklamakan and Gobi deserts to connect their respective railway systems. This was to fall victim to their later disagreements and was left unfinished for over 30 years. Recently the railway has been completed and it is by virtue of these efforts that this remarkable journey is made possible. Although the journey is principally by special train, overnight stops in hotels are

A Journey along the Silk Route

made in Peking, Xian and, according to your chosen itinerary Kashgar, Naryn, Bishket or Alma Ata. The arrangement represents extremely good value in that it is fully inclusive of all transportation, accommodation, meals and comprehensive sightseeing programme.

THE SPECIAL TRAIN

For this journey we have reserved what the Chinese refer to as the 'China Orient Express', a train that was constructed in the 1950s for the government elite and later for diplomats in which to travel. Normally the train comprises seven sleeping carriages each with eight compartments with each two compartments sharing a separate vestibule for washing and hand-held shower facility. The twin-berth compartments contain a table and a living area for daytime travel. Dependent on the number of travellers there are two air-conditioned restaurants and club car. Sleeping compartments have fans.

ITINERARY

DAY 1 Depart London Heathrow on the overnight flight to Tashkent.

DAY 2 On arrival connect with the regional flight to Bishket, the capital of Kirghizia, for an overnight stay.

DAY 3 Continue by road to Lake Issyk Kul with its aquamarine stillness, arrive in Naryn in the afternoon.

DAY 4 Today we are in the region of the explorer as we travel south east to the Tianshan Mountains to the Chinese border at Turugart Pass and then on to the fabled oasis outpost of the 'Great Game', Kashgar.

DAY 5 Kashgar is a fine example of one of China's little known facets: its Islamic history. First brought under Chinese dominion in 200BC, it became a Muslim centre during the 10th century. Visits will be arranged to the Abakh Hoja tomb the great Id Kah mosque fronted by the Bust Square.

DAY 6 Depart Kashgar by air to Urumchi where our special train will be waiting to take us on the first leg of our journey through the Gobi Desert in the direction of Turfan.

DAY 7 Pass through some spectacular scenery and arrive at the oasis town of Turfan. During our stay visit both the Flaming Mountains and the ancient city of Gauchang before reboarding our train for our journey through the night.

DAY 8 Arrive at Liuyang just after breakfast and here we alight for a two hour journey through the Gobi to visit the 10,000 Buddha Grottoes of Dunhuang. Overnight in Dunhuang.

DAY 9 Return to our train and continue to the southernmost part of the Great Wall at the Jiayuguan Pass where our train will make a short stop so that we may make a visit before proceeding through the Gobi towards Lanzhan.

DAY 10 Cross the Yellow River, the so called cradle of Chinese civilisation, after breakfast and continuing eastwards through the night.

DAY 11 Arrive at the terminus of the Silk Route at Chang'an or Xian as it is known today. Here we will spend two days visiting the major sights including the Wild Goose Pagoda and the famous Terracotta Warriors just outside the city.

DAY 12 Further sightseeing and after an evening Tang Dynasty banquet we rejoin our train for the journey through the night towards Luoyang.

DAY 13 Arrive Luoyang and after a comprehensive visit to the many sights we continue our train journey northwards towards Peking.

DAY 14 Arrive Peking in the morning and transfer to the hotel for a two night stay. During the stay visits will be made to the Forbidden City, the Great Wall and the Ming Tombs.

DAY 15 Further exploration of Peking and its environs with optional visits to the Summer Palace, Peking Zoo or the Temple of Heaven.

DAY 16 Depart in the morning on the British Airways Boeing 747 flight to London Heathrow arriving the same day.

0171-616 1000

VOYAGES JULES VERNE
21 Dorset Square,
London NW1
Travel Promotions Ltd.
ABTA V1661 ATOL 883B

Our offices are open for telephone reservations from 9am to 8pm weekdays and from 9am to 5pm at the weekends, For personal visitors our office hours are 9am to 5pm weekdays only.

Higher Level – Questions — A Journey along the Silk Route

Time: _____

Read the advertisement, then answer the questions.

1. From the first paragraph, find four advantages in travelling by train through part of China.
   (4 marks)

2. From the second paragraph, quote one fact and one opinion expressed by the advertisers.
   (2 marks)

3. Which days actually involve being on the train?
   (2 marks)

4. Mention three features of this advertisement that help in presenting the facts to the reader. *(6 marks)*

5. Why do you think the trip is not described as a holiday? Give at least two reasons.
   (4 marks)

Answer one question below:

6a. Using information from any three consecutive days of the itinerary, write a letter home describing what you have experienced. You may use your imagination to make the letter lively and interesting but you must make suitable reference to the advert's information.
   (20 marks)

6b. What do you feel are the advantages and disadvantages of people visiting far off places that have not been developed for tourists? Consider the question not only from the tourist's point of view but also from the point of view of those who live in these locations.
   (20 marks)

6c. Imagine you have just returned from the Silk Route journey. You have been asked to write an article for a magazine on advice for travellers who visit China. Your advice should deal with what to see and also cover precautions and safety.
   (20 marks)

A Journey along the Silk Route   Higher Level – Answers

A Journey along the Silk Route Marking Suggestions   Advised Time: 1 hour

1. From the first paragraph, find four advantages in travelling by train through part of China. *(4 marks)*
   - *visits are easier to accomplish*
   - *more comfortable*
   - *less expensive*
   - *'a chance to get off the well-trodden tourist track'.*

2. From the second paragraph quote one fact and one opinion expressed by the advertisers. *(2 marks)*
   - *fact, any of the historical details*
   - *opinion, the last sentence, 'the arrangement represents extremely good value for money.'*

3. Which days actually involve being on the train? *(2 marks)*
   - *day 6*
   - *to day 14.*

4. Mention three presentation features of this advertisement that help in presenting the facts to the reader. *(6 marks, 2 marks for each explained feature)*
   - *the itinerary (organisation of the trip) is broken down into the events for each day*
   - *a summary of the journey is presented in large letters under the main picture*
   - *the picture depicts what the traveller will see*
   - *other pieces of information, such as prices are given sub-headings.*

5. Why do you think the trip is not described as a holiday? Give at least two reasons. *(4 marks – up to 2 marks for each explanation)*
   - *the word holiday might cheapen the importance and exclusivity of the journey*
   - *the package is presented as an adventure with a busy list of visits and sight-seeing. There is an educational element to the journey*
   - *a holiday would imply a relaxing and undemanding time.*

6a. Using information from any three consecutive days of the itinerary, write a letter home describing what you have experienced. You may use your imagination to make the letter lively and interesting but you must make suitable reference to the advert's information. *(20 marks)*

   20 – 16 Answers will contain a majority of these points:
   - *correct letter layout*
   - *marks for creating an appropriate address from the sender*
   - *the tone will be chatty but there is reference throughout the letter to events mentioned in the itinerary*
   - *there will be imagination and empathy with conditions on the train and the people they are encountering from the fellow travellers to the local Chinese*
   - *answers may make reference to the complexities of the language and the difference in culture*
   - *technically excellent with confident use of punctuation and few, if any, spelling errors.*

   15 – 11 Answers will contain a majority of these points:
   - *correct letter layout*
   - *a suitable tone for writing to friends or family*
   - *less reference to the material and the use of it to provide the imaginative response*
   - *opinions on what they have 'seen' will be superficial judgements, e.g. 'the train was crowded'*
   - *technically good with a varied vocabulary.*

   10 – 6 Answers will contain a majority of these points:
   - *correct letter layout*
   - *the tone is likely to be chatty and there may be too much emphasis on how the receiver is keeping, e.g. 'are you all well, have you got over your cold?'*
   - *reference to the itinerary is brief, factual and under-used*
   - *the lower end of this band for those who use copied sentences that have few if any additional comments*
   - *expression is fair but the vocabulary is limited and the work has a noticeable number of technical errors.*

   5 or under Answers will contain a majority of these points:
   - *days may not be consecutive or the letter might refer to the whole holiday*
   - *reference to the itinerary is superficial*
   - *there is little sense of understanding what it is like to travel in a very different place*
   - *noticeable technical errors and a poor structure to the piece.*

6b. What do you feel are the advantages and disadvantages of people visiting far off places that have not been developed for tourists? Consider the question not only from the tourist's point of view but also from the point of view of those who live in these locations. *(20 marks)*

   20 – 16 Answers will contain a majority of these points:
   - *well-organised work that looks at a number of aspects and keeps close to the question*
   - *the argument does not have to be balanced but there should be consideration from both angles*
   - *points will be explained well and many will be backed up with examples*
   - *reference will be made to the advertisement such as the journey deliberately going off the tourist*

- route and visiting holy shrines
- expression is confident with few, if any, technical errors at the top end of this band.

15 – 11 Answers will contain a majority of these points:
- fair organisation although points may not have been presented in the best order
- less balance to the argument, there may be little consideration of the locals' view of intrusive tourists
- there will be a need for more examples to support opinions
- some reference to the advertisement
- good expression but vocabulary is more limited than top band work
- a more limited range of punctuation and some spelling errors.

10 – 6 Answers will contain a majority of these points:
- some organisation but points are likely to be presented as they occurred to the writer
- little development of ideas and few, if any, examples to support opinions
- an unbalanced argument that may not consider the locals
- fair but repetitive expression
- noticeable errors in punctuation and spelling.

5 or below Answers will contain a majority of these points:
- unorganised work with random ideas
- unoriginal thinking and opinionated views with no examples
- noticeable errors that may hamper the expression.

6c. Imagine you have just returned from the Silk Route journey. You have been asked to write an article for a magazine on advice for travellers who visit China. Your advice should deal with what to see and also cover precautions and safety. *(20 marks)*

20 – 16 marks Answers will contain a majority of these points:
- awareness of the magazine style in layout and approach so there should be a heading, sub-titles and there may be feature boxes e.g. 'Don't forget to take …'
- magazine style in tone, language is informal but not slangy, helpful, possibly using the question and answer technique such as 'what should I take?'
- a good choice of features to see from the advertisement but in their own words
- well structured
- a good balance between both aspects of the question – what to see and what to be aware of
- ideas are sensible with a good perception of the problems of travelling in China such as language, customs and expectations
- technically excellent with confident use of punctuation and few, if any, spelling errors. Punctuation, particularly paragraphing may be over-used to emulate the magazine style.

15 - 11 Answers will contain a majority of these points:
- awareness of the magazine style in layout and approach, there should at least be a headline
- a suitable tone for the audience, still a sense that it 'speaks' to the reader
- good use of the advertisement for names of places and features to see but …
- there may be an imbalance in both parts of question with too much reliance on what to see
- some structure to the piece but points may not be presented in the best order
- a varied vocabulary
- technically good, few spelling mistakes with familiar words. Punctuation is good at the top end of this band.

10 - 6 Answers will contain a majority of these points:
- the piece might seem more like an essay for a teacher than an article
- good ideas mentioned but possibly repeated or over-explained
- over or under use of the advertisement, particularly if most features of the 16 day trip are copied out
- advice is likely to be superficial e.g. put your name on your luggage, and the fact that the journey is in China has not been thought through
- some structure to the piece but the ideas are not in the best order
- the piece is under developed probably due to bad time management
- a pedestrian vocabulary
- some punctuation might be misplaced and spelling is noticeable as a problem.

5 or below Answers will contain a majority of these points:
- a misunderstanding of the task
- wrong tone
- poor expression
- few or no examples
- no discernible structure
- technically weak with frequent errors
- marks at this level would fail the student in this section.

Guide to grade boundaries:	
38 – 35	A*
34 – 31	A
30 – 27	B
26 – 23	C
22 – 19	D
Below 19	U

Happy Christmas?

MY ONE and only appearance on Radio 4's ill-fated *Anderson Country* was about this time last year, when I was approached to contribute to a piece about the joys of Christmas with a grown-up family. It was a disaster. I had to talk to a disembodied voice from London in a tiny booth in the BBC's studio in charismatic Ipswich. All my attempts to be amusing and light-hearted failed and I came across as a grumpy old kill-joy. The *coup de grace* coming when Anderson said 'And it's over to Mr Ransom, in Suffolk, for the final word' and I heard myself saying 'Forget Christmas! It's a pain in the neck as far as I'm concerned'.

I was never paid the promised fee and I hadn't the heart to chase it. My family shunned me for days afterwards, and so you can see why my foray into radio humour was a disaster. The idea was to contrast Christmasses when the children were young, the fun and excitement of hanging stockings, the magic of Father Christmas, and the delightful innocence of it all, with the agony and sweat of Christmas with those same children, who have to all intents and purposes grown up, but who have not yet flown the nest. Take the business of the stocking. Years ago it was dead easy. You bunged a tangerine, some nuts and a Mars bar in a sock, and the kids loved it. You crept into their bedrooms at a reasonable hour and even though you might be wakened at six o'clock in the morning, the bouncing around on the parental bed, in a sea of wrapping paper, was always enjoyable. It's all so different when they get older.

When we decided our kids had grown out of stockings they were horrified. Not only did they insist on stockings but they had to be the ones we had always used. But it's not easy. For a start you can't creep into their bedrooms without turning your ankle on the piles of shoes and clothes strewn on the floor. Compact disc boxes crunch under your feet and the reek of unwashed clothes, alcohol and sweat make you gasp for air, let alone the fear that if the semi-comatose form were to stir, you might be accused of child molestation. And it's so late! Our youth always "go out" on Christmas Eve, ending with Midnight Mass, so you fret about until after one o'clock, knowing they're bound to have had a drink or six, fearing disgrace befalling the entire family as a result of their one and only contact with the church all year. You not only have to keep awake until they stagger home, but you have to wait until they've had a last fag, another drink, and a mince pie. Chastisement is out of the question at this stage of the festivities.

The following morning there is not a sound from the young, except the thump of Radio One which has been left on all night. Meanwhile anxious parents get up early to put the turkey in the Aga. Breakfast is a non-event. Just as you've cleared the table one bleary eyed youth will appear and grizzle because his or her croissant has gone cold. The moment you've cleared up after the first child, a second will appear demanding breakfast. It's no fun any more, as I tried to say to Anderson, but then after church someone will say how nice it was to see the children at Midnight Mass and you begin to wonder. Do I need counselling, or parenting training? I blame it all on that Anderson bloke. If he hadn't asked me I'd never have given it a thought.

David Ransom, Oldie, December 1996

> **You not only have to keep awake until they stagger home, but you have to wait until they've had a last fag, another drink, and a mince pie**

Higher Level – Questions

Happy Christmas?

Time: _____

Read the article "Happy Christmas?" and answer the questions.

Note to students: This article was published in a magazine called The Oldie, a general interest humour magazine. Anderson Country was an afternoon radio programme that discussed topical issues, often with a humorous slant.

1. The third sentence in the first paragraph of Happy Christmas suggests three reasons why David Ransom's broadcast was "a disaster". In your own words explain these reasons. *(3 marks)*

2. How do we know that the bedrooms of the author's children are untidy? *(3 marks)*

3. How old do you think the author's children are? Give careful reasons, including any points which seem to make it hard to come to an exact answer. *(5 marks)*

4. The author frequently exaggerates. Give examples of this and other times when you do not think he really means what he says. Explain what effect you think David Ransom is trying to achieve. *(5 marks)*

Answer one question below

5a. Write a diary entry by one of David Ransom's children giving their account of Christmas Eve now compared to when they were much younger. *(20 marks)*

5b. Write a letter of complaint by a listener in response to David Ransom's contribution to Radio Four's Anderson Country. *(20 marks)*

5c. Write a script of a conversation between one of David Ransom's children and David Ransom's wife on the subject of his (David Ransom's) sense of humour. *(20 marks)*

Happy Christmas? Marking Suggestions

Advised Time: 60/75 minutes

1. The third sentence in the first paragraph of Happy Christmas suggests three reasons why David Ransom's broadcast was "a disaster". In your own words explain these reasons. *(3 marks)*
   - he couldn't see the person he was talking to ("...to whom he was talking" if we have to be picky)
   - the intended point is presumably, he was in a small and confined space, but allow, the author was made nervous by being in a BBC studio, which is possible. If both these points are made, then the following point is not needed.
   - the term "charismatic Ipswich" is ironic/sarcastic. The author presumably means that Ipswich is so dull that it is hard to be witty when speaking from there.

2. How do we know that the author's children's bedrooms are untidy? *(3 marks)*
   - shoes and clothes left on the floor
   - CD cases left on the floor
   - the smell, coming from dirty clothes, alcohol and sweat.

3. How old do you think the author's children are? Give careful reasons, including any points which seem to make it hard to decide. *(5 marks)*
   No marks for a particular age, but up to four for supporting whatever choice is made (if one is) with relevant evidence, and the fifth mark for pointing out that the evidence is contradictory.
   - "...to all intents and purposes grown up, but who have not yet flown the nest" - suggests old (e.g. 17+?) but
   - insisting on using stockings for their presents (and the same old ones,) suggests childishness, as does
   - "child molestation" even though this is not meant seriously
   - the fact that the author as father accepts them drinking heavily "a drink or six" and smoking ("a last fag") suggests old, but
   - to "grizzle" because of a cold croissant is childish
   - the use of terms is also contradictory, with "youth" sounding much older than "child" or "kids".

4. The author frequently exaggerates. Give examples of this and other times when you do not think he really means what he says. Explain what effect you think David Ransom is trying to achieve. *(5 marks)*
   Impossible to be exhaustive, so teachers' discretion required, but some possibilities include:
   - the programme does sound a "disaster", but students could point out that real disasters (such as earthquakes, volcanoes etc.) involve loss of life and widespread destruction, and that Ransom is thus trying to show how bad this experience was
   - he is either exaggerating the meanness of his presents to his young children "tangerine, nuts and a Mars bar" or else he is certainly exaggerating their response "the kids loved it." His point is to show how easy it was to give pleasure to his children at Christmas when they were small. Very able students might even pick up on the use of the word "bunged" to show how little effort was required
   - sea of wrapping paper - a straightforward metaphor to show the visual impact (which would only be achieved by unwrapping rather more than a tangerine, some nuts and a Mars bar)
   - Ransom exaggerates several aspects of the problems of placing the presents in his older children's bedrooms. These include details of the untidiness of their bedrooms, the notion of being accused of child molestation
   - the idea that their behaviour in church would lead to disgrace for the whole family seems exaggerated.

Answer one question below:
N.B. These questions require close reading of the article, but they are also creative and notwithstanding the criteria listed below, high marks can be awarded for work that is sufficiently original and interesting to read.

5a. Write a diary entry by one of David Ransom's children giving their account of Christmas Eve now compared to when they were much younger. *(20 marks)*
   20-16 Answers will contain a majority of these points:
   - an appropriate form of language for a diary
   - an appropriate tone, not just for a diary, but given the subject matter, probably an ironic/sardonic tone commenting on the father
   - probably some comment on their Dad's sense of humour, which they are unlikely to appreciate
   - a reference to the fact that the old tradition of present-giving is retained, either a confirmation of their Dad's view that this is at their insistence, or the opposite, that they feel they have outgrown it and their father insists on retaining it
   - some reference to show their grown-up habits, drinking, smoking, what they feel about going to Midnight Mass
   - the difficulty of getting a decent breakfast on Christmas morning
   - technically very good at the top end with few errors.

   15-11 Answers will contain a majority of these points:
   - a clear understanding that this is meant to be a diary entry, even if some of the forms are not wholly appropriate
   - clearly written from the point of view of one of David Ransom's children, though the tone may not be consistent. It might be too angry or an attempt at humour may not quite come off
   - there will be reference to the rituals of giving presents then and now, but it might not be wholly clear what the writer's point of view is with regard to these changes
   - technically fair but there may be common and repeated errors.
   Penalise mis-spellings of words that are in the article

Higher Level – Answers

Happy Christmas?

10-6 Answers will contain a majority of these points:
- some notion that this is a diary, but possible confusion about who is writing the piece (e.g. switches between third and first person)
- possible overlong quotation or inappropriate references to the article (such as to the radio programme) but...
- no extension of any of the points from the article
- little sense of comparison between Christmasses when they were little and now
- technically weak although the mistakes do not hamper the overall meaning.

5 or less Answers will contain a majority of these points:
- very little if any sense of a diary entry
- confusion as to who is writing
- little if any comparison between Christmasses past and present
- possible overlong and unassimilated quotation
- very weak technically.

5b. Write a letter of complaint by a listener in response to David Ransom's contribution to Radio Four's Anderson Country. *(20 marks)*

20-16 Answers will contain a majority of these points:
- accurate use of the conventions of a formal letter
- appropriate tone and vocabulary for a keen radio listener
- an expansion of Ransom's own evaluation that he came across as a grumpy old kill-joy
- particular reference to his last comment, "Forget Christmas..."
- a derogatory verdict on his attempts at humour
- appropriate use of the clues from the rest of the article as to what else he actually said on the programme
- technically accurate, with very few mistakes at the top end.

15-11 Answers will contain a majority of these points:
- an attempt to use the conventions of a formal letter
- an attempt at a formal tone and vocabulary
- some appropriate use of the contents of the rest of the article
- complaints about the content, without necessarily recognising the attempts at humour
- a reference to his last comment
- technically fair but there may be common and repeated errors.

Penalise mis-spellings of words that are in the article.

10-6 Answers will contain a majority of these points:
- the use of a letter form though not necessarily that of a formal letter
- an inconsistent tone, with intrusions of inappropriately informal language
- complaints about the content of the programme may include information from the rest of the article not reprocessed to suggest it was actually included in the programme
- technically weak, but meaning comes through.

5 or below Answers will contain a majority of these points:
- not a successful use of the letter form
- no recognisable attempt at formal language
- short and not using the information in the article
- technically weak.

5c. Write a script of a conversation between one of David Ransom's children and David Ransom's wife on the subject of his sense of humour. *(20 marks)*

20-16 Answers will contain a majority of these points:
- a consistent use of the conventions of scriptwriting (eg name of character in margin, no speech marks use of brackets for stage directions)
- appropriate use of informal, (spoken) registers. The most able students will create a different 'voice' for Ransom's wife and her son/daughter, which may reflect their different ages
- intelligent use of information in the passage - such as Ransom's habit of exaggerating. There is no necessity for either party to have fixed points of view on this topic i.e. it is not a requirement for the wife to defend and the 'child' to attack the sense of humour
- a high level of technical accuracy.

15-11 Answers will contain a majority of these points:
- a basically accurate attempt to use the script format
- a largely successful attempt to represent spoken language
- some use of the content of the article - e.g. mention of the radio programme and recognition of its shortcomings
- technically fair but there may be common and repeated errors.

Penalise mis-spellings of words that are in the article.

10-6 Answers will contain a majority of these points:
- an attempt to use the script format
- an attempt, but not consistent at appropriate informal language
- some effort to use the information in the article
- technically weak but not hindering comprehension.

5 or less Answers will contain a majority of these points:
- not a successful use of the script format
- no recognisable attempt at appropriate informal language
- short and not using the information in the article
- technically weak.

Guide to grade boundaries	
For questions 1-4	
16 - 15	A*
14 - 13	A
12 - 11	B
10 - 9	C
8 - 7	D
6 or below	U
For question 5	
20 - 18	A*
17 - 16	A
15 - 14	B
13 - 12	C
11 - 10	D
9 or below	U

winning smiles

When Susan Duncan appeared on television, her courage touched the hearts of millions. She talks about living with facial disfigurement

"I have been facially disfigured since the age of two when I had a cancerous tumour removed from my face. It took with it my palate, cheekbone and upper jaw on the left side."

In books and films, beauty has traditionally represented good, and evil has been portrayed by scarred and disfigured beings who lead reclusive lives. I fit neither of these descriptions.

Susan Duncan holding the 'Great Scot' award for unsung heroes.

There is a lot of stigma attached to being facially disfigured in a society which is obsessed with beauty and appearance. Every day of my life when I walk down the street, people stare at me and make comments as if I cannot see or hear them. Generally I let it wash over me, it's pointless to provoke confrontation, but it doesn't mean I accept being treated like this.

I grew up with my facial disfigurement and went to an ordinary school, loving every minute of it and gaining a good education and qualifications. I never realised that I would be subjected to discrimination and prejudice if I wanted to have a successful career. It has not been easy trying to balance a career and years of surgery to reconstruct my face.

There are laws to protect against most types of discrimination but none to protect me - I often get asked questions about my appearance at job interviews. On paper I am good enough to be short-listed for interview, but when some prospective employers meet me face-to-face, things change. Perhaps they are not aware that they are putting up a barrier and refusing to see beyond the disfigurement.

Nevertheless I get on with my life. It can be lonely. You may say: "We don't see many facially disfigured people." That's true, but they do exist. Some of them choose not to put up with the reactions they get from this cruel, image conscious society and stay out of the public view. I can understand why. But I also know it can be difficult for people when they meet someone with a disfigurement.

When I was asked if I would take part in a documentary for QED, I welcomed the opportunity with open arms. It was a daunting prospect but it was also the challenge I had been waiting for. And it was an excellent opportunity to dispel some of the misconceptions people have about facial disfigurement.

It is caused by a variety of things like burns, cancer or accidents, and treatment can be a long, slow and painful process. It is devastating to find that your appearance has changed, and to have to live with that. That is why there is a desperate need for psychological support and counselling in conjunction with plastic surgery units.

> "On paper I am good enough to be short-listed for interview, but when prospective employers meet me face-to-face, things change"

From the positive response to the QED programme, I think it has gone some way to helping viewers understand what disfigurement is like. I got hundreds of letters from all over the country, from doctors, actresses and just ordinary people who said the programme made them think. I even got a couple from men asking me on dates! I also got letters from people who are disfigured, saying that I had said what they had always wanted to say. A lot of people came up to me in the street after the programme. They still do, and I'm glad. People who would have just stared now smile at me."

The Big Issue

Winning Smiles

£55,000 BODY When money's the root of all beauty...

Cindy: before the knife

Come the next century, going under the knife to improve our looks will be as common as buying a designer suit.

In 1994 48,000 cosmetic surgery operations were carried out in the UK, and the market is currently expanding at a rate of eight per cent per year.

Londoner Cindy Jackson epitomises the way people will use plastic surgery in the future. She has had over 20 operations, re-designing herself from head to toe.

Cindy holds the world record for plastic surgery. She's spent £55,000 and endured eight painful years of operations.

Now aged 41 she has opted for a Barbie Doll look: "It pushes all the right buttons," she claims. "Ask any anthropologist and they'll tell you that the traits that encourage the nurturing instinct are big eyes, small noses, full lips and soft skin."

- To achieve her look she chose Christy Brinkley's eyes, Elle MacPherson's nose, Claudia Schiffer's cheekbones and Julia Robert's mouth.

- Beginning with an operation to have her jaws widened, she then had liposuction on her jawline, abdomen, knees and thighs, followed by a face-lift, two chemical peels, silicone breast implants and three nose jobs. She has had cosmetic dentistry, chin reduction, laser resurfacing and cheek implants.

Cindy Jackson's new face has cost her over £45,000

Liposuction on knees, thighs and abdomen. Breast implants: £7950

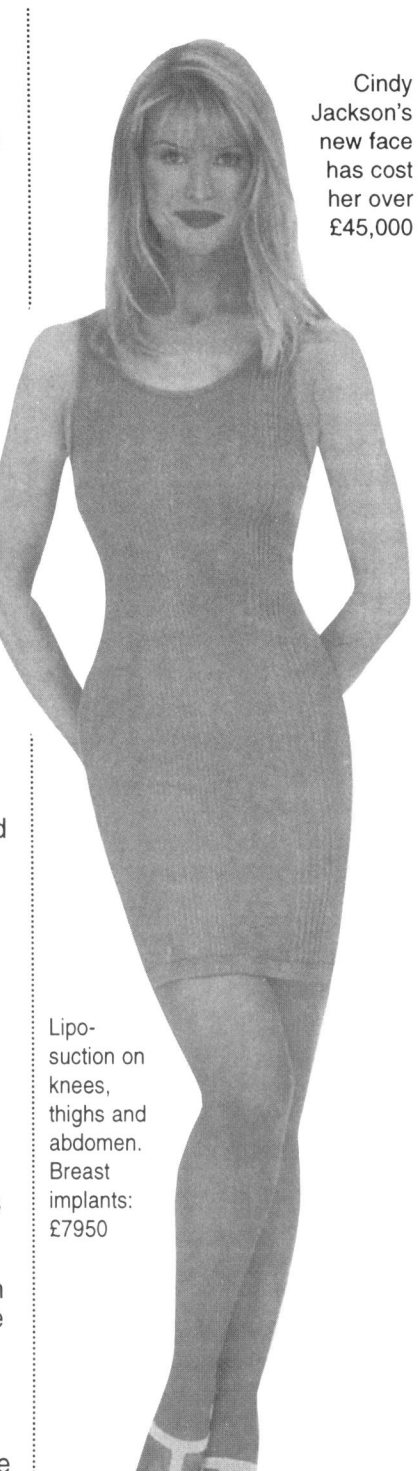

- Cindy decided to start over again at 31, after inheriting money from her father.

"I was tired of leading a mediocre existence," she says. "I wanted a glamorous life and decided to equip myself with the tools to achieve it.

"Now I can cross a street whenever I want because male drivers will always stop to look at my figure. I call the shots and relish my power."

- Numerous studies demonstrate that attractive people fare best in all situations. They make more friends and more money and have sex with more partners. In the workplace, attractive people tend to have accelerated career paths. They even get lighter jail sentences.

- But even so, will the British public be tempted *en masse*? Perhaps. Developments in anaesthesia will end the fear of pain, while keyhole surgery will mean less scarring.

And in future, patients themselves could redesign the way they look. Images created by two-dimensional computed tomography (CT) scans will be fed into a program to produce a 3-D head with which you could try out different styles of noses, eyelids, chins or lips.

- Ultimately technology may do away with the knife altogether. Charing Cross Hospital surgeon Dai Davies forecasts that gene therapy will one day enable doctors to slow down the ageing process, by extracting genes from people who have naturally aged slowly and 'infecting' others with them.

Focus

Winning Smiles

Foundation Level – Questions

Time: _____

Read the article "When money's the root of all beauty" and answer all of the questions that follow.

1. How much have Cindy's operations cost?
   (1 mark)

2. Name six operations Cindy has had on her face.
   (6 marks)

3. Look at the third bullet point which begins '• Cindy decided to start over again at 31 ...'. What does Cindy mean by the line, 'I call the shots and relish my power'?
   (2 marks)

4. Comment on the layout of this article and what features make it interesting.
   (6 marks)

Now read the article, "Winning Smiles" and use both articles to help you with the next question.

Answer one question below.

5a. Imagine a television debate where Cindy and Susan have been asked to discuss their attitude to beauty. Write how you think the conversation might sound in the form of a script. You could cast yourself as the interviewer.
   (20 marks)

or

5b. You are the editor of a problem page for a teenage magazine and have received a number of letters from teenagers who are very depressed about their looks. Reply to their letters with some helpful advice. Do not write the letters from the teenagers, just suitable replies.
   (20 marks)

or

5c. A charity has asked for your school's support to raise awareness of facial disfigurement. You have been asked to present a talk to people in your year about this issue and to give some ideas about how your school could help. Write the talk that you would give to the students.
   (20 marks)

Foundation Level – Answers

Winning Smiles

Winning Smiles and When money's the root of all beauty Marking Suggestions
Advised time 60 / 75 minutes.

1. How much have Cindy's operations cost?
   (1 mark)
   - **£55,000**

2. Name six operations Cindy has had on her face.
   (6 marks - one for each up to six)
   - *her jaw widened*
   - *liposuction on her jawline*
   - *a face lift*
   - *three nose jobs*
   - *chin reduction*
   - *cheek implants*
   - *laser resurfacing*
   - *cosmetic dentistry*
   - *chemical peels*

   (You may want to deduct a mark for non-facial operations mentioned.)

3. Look at the third bullet point which begins '• Cindy decided to start over again at 31 …'. What does Cindy mean by the line, 'I call the shots and relish my power'? *(2 marks)*
   - *something similar to, 'I make the decisions in my life and I enjoy this control'.*

4. Comment on the layout of this article and what features make it interesting.
   (6 marks - students may comment on:)
   - *eye-catching picture dividing the text*
   - *two pictures of Cindy looking confidently at the reader*
   - *the 'price tag' commentary next to her picture*
   - *the '£55,000 Body' in the top left corner*
   - *short, bulleted paragraphs*
   - *clear and simply expressed facts.*

5a. Imagine a television debate where Cindy and Susan have been asked to discuss their attitude to beauty. Write how you think the conversation might sound in the form of a script. You could cast yourself as the interviewer.

   20 - 16 Answers will contain a majority of these points:
   - *a script layout or a clear structure so it is clear who is speaking*
   - *well-drawn evidence from the two articles*
   - *a good sense of Susan's attitude to her disfigurement*
   - *creative empathy with Cindy's attitude*
   - *a lively response between the two characters such as one woman responding to the other's comments*
   - *some progression in the argument, points are not repeated*
   - *the programme should be introduced in a suitable style*
   - *spelling good and careful use of punctuation, few errors.*

   15- 11 Answers will contain a majority of these points:
   - *a script layout or a clear structure so it is clear who is speaking*
   - *both sides of the argument expressed through the women but it may be unbalanced in favour of one*
   - *ideas drawn from the articles but not always capitalized on*
   - *less structure to the overall piece and good arguments in inappropriate places or not elaborated on*
   - *an opening to the programme*
   - *technically fair at the top end of this band but more noticeable errors in spelling and punctuation.*

   10 - 6 Answers will contain a majority of these points:
   - *bad planning means characters don't have an equal opportunity to justify their view*
   - *comments are superficial or very brief*
   - *the piece should still be in the form of a script*
   - *technically weak in places with errors in punctuation and some simple words (for the lower end of this band).*

   5 or below
   - *likely to have misunderstood the task*
   - *it may not read as a script*
   - *Susan and Cindy do not seem like the people in the articles.*

5b. You are the editor of a problem page for a teenage magazine and have received a number of letters from teenagers who are very depressed about their looks. Reply to their letters with some helpful advice. Do not write the letters from the teenagers, just suitable replies.

   20 - 16 Answers will contain a majority of these points:
   - *appropriate tone that speaks to the readers in a friendly and helpful way*

Winning Smiles
Foundation Level – Answers

- advice is sensible bearing in mind the writer is a teenager
- some reference to the articles
- good planning so that the advice is presented in a helpful and ordered way
- a good range of expression
- spelling good and careful use of punctuation. Very few errors.

15 - 11 Answers will contain a majority of these points:
- a suitable tone that communicates with the readers but less subtle than the above criteria
- points not in the best order
- at least one reference to the articles
- probably too many replies have been attempted so the work is more superficial
- technically fair at the top end of this band but more noticeable errors in spelling and punctuation.

10 - 6 Answers will contain a majority of these points:
- the student might have included letters from teenagers despite the instructions
- advice is likely to be superficial and unplanned or helpful but badly expressed
- technically weak in places with errors in punctuation and some simple words (for the lower end of this band).

5 or below
- a misunderstanding of the task such as writing a letter to the magazine
- possibly very short work or repetitive in content
- tone unsuitable for a teenage magazine
- technical errors may hamper the understanding.

5c. A charity has asked for your school's support to raise awareness of facial disfigurement. You have been asked to present a talk to people in your year about this issue and to give some ideas about how your school could help. Write the talk that you would give to the students.

20 - 16 Answers will contain a majority of these points:
- an organised talk with an introduction, series of points and conclusion
- an interesting plan of action with a variety of ideas highlighting who their campaign will target

- useful references to the Winning Smiles article
- a suitable tone, conversational but not too informal, the very best will employ speech techniques such as rhetorical questions
- good expression, the tone is not repetitive
- spelling good and careful use of punctuation, very few errors.

15 - 11 Answers will contain a majority of these points:
- some structure to the talk although the best points may be misplaced
- some ideas may be limited or repetitive or ideas are promising but not fully developed
- at least one reference to the Winning Smiles article
- more limited in the range of expression
- technically fair at the top end of this band but more noticeable errors in spelling and punctuation.

10 - 6 Answers will contain a majority of these points:
- the talk is not structured but just a series of ideas not in the best order
- a few ideas although they are not explained well or not developed
- the tone is repetitive and unlikely to read like a talk for students
- expression is limited
- inappropriate, if any, use of the Winning Smiles article
- technically weak in places with errors in punctuation and some simple words (for the lower end of this band).

5 or below
- the item has not been thought through and will not achieve what the question asked
- technical errors throughout the piece.

Guide to grade boundaries:	
35 - 31	C
30 - 26	D
25 - 21	E
20 - 16	F
15 - 11	G
Below 11	U

Time: _____

Read the articles "Winning Smiles" and "When money's the root of all beauty." Answer the questions.

1. From the first two paragraphs of "Winning Smiles", what facts are we given about Susan Duncan? *(3 marks)*

2. In your own words explain some of the problems Susan Duncan has had to overcome. *(3 marks)*

3. What overall benefits to the public have come from the QED programme? *(3 marks)*

4. Comment on how the two articles have made careful use of the photographs. *(6 marks)*

5. Select and explain three features in Susan Duncan's article that make it interesting to the reader. *(6 marks)*

Answer one question below.

6a. Imagine a television debate where Cindy and Susan have been asked to discuss their attitude to beauty. Write the conversation in the form of a script, casting yourself as the interviewer.
(20 marks)

or

6b. Using evidence from the two articles and your own ideas, write an essay on the advantages and disadvantages of being beautiful.
(20 marks)

or

6c. A charity concerned with discrimination because of facial disfigurement has written a letter to a number of employers trying to educate them on the facts of this issue and urging them to change their attitude. Either write this letter or write the reply from one hotel chain that may not agree with the charity's arguments.
(20 marks)

Winning Smiles

Higher Level – Answers

Winning Smiles and When money's the root of all beauty Marking Suggestions
Advised time – 75 minutes.

1. From the first two paragraphs of "Winning Smiles" what facts are we given about Susan Duncan? *(3 marks)*
   Note: The second paragraph is all opinions.
   - *facially disfigured since two years old*
   - *cancerous tumour was removed*
   - *she lost her palate, cheekbone and upper jaw*
   (at least two of these should be mentioned)

2. In your own words explain some of the problems Susan Duncan has had to overcome.
   (up to 3 marks)
   - *people stare and make comments as if she is deaf or blind*
   - *discrimination at job interviews*
   - *loneliness*
   - *stigma: association of disfigurement with evil, 'beauty has traditionally represented good'*
   - *the years of surgery while trying to develop a career.*

3. What overall benefits to the public (not specifically to Susan) have come from the QED programme? *(3 marks)*
   - *helping viewers understand disfigurement, it made them think*
   - *'dispelling some of the misconceptions'*
   - *changing people's attitude*
   - *helping people to express their feelings.*

4. Comment on how the two articles have made careful use of the photographs.
   (up to 6 marks - a well-explained point could gain two marks)
   - *photo of Susan holding an award*
   - *her disfigurement clearly shown*
   - *contrasting pictures of Cindy, before and after the operations*
   - *picture of Cindy and her body shape dominates the article*
   - *Cindy staring confidently at the reader*

5. Select and explain three features in Susan Duncan's article that make it interesting to the reader. *(up to 6 marks - a well-explained point could gain two marks)*
   - *told in the first person, an honest and frank view*
   - *a subject that is not often written about*
   - *lots of examples*
   - *the style is conversational and the language not complex.*

6a. Imagine a television debate where Cindy and Susan have been asked to discuss their attitude to beauty. Write the conversation in the form of a script, casting yourself as the interviewer.

   20 - 16 Answers will contain a majority of these points:
   - *excellent evidence drawn from the two articles*
   - *a sense of 'knowing' the personalities of the two women and realising the motivation of Cindy to undergo all the surgery and the strength of Susan to withstand the attitudes of other people*
   - *lively expression*
   - *a good structure to the piece*
   - *the conversation develops their individual viewpoints*
   - *a clear layout, we can identify who is speaking*
   - *few, if any, technical errors.*

   15 - 11 Answers will contain a majority of these points:
   - *good use of the two articles, possibly using words the two women have used*
   - *the style of the two speakers is likely to be less subtle and understanding, at the lower end they may 'talk' much in the same voice*
   - *a series of points are made as opposed to discussing the issue*
   - *a clear layout, we can identify who is speaking*
   - *technically good, few errors in punctuation and spelling.*

   10 - 6 Answers will contain a majority of these points:
   - *points taken from both articles but not developed so the responses from the women are brief*
   - *both women express themselves in the same way, limited expression*
   - *poor planning with a possible bias to one of the articles*
   - *a clear layout, we can identify who is speaking*
   - *technically fair but noticeable errors throughout the piece.*

   5 or below
   As above but many more technical errors, poor planning and a limited empathy with either situation.

Higher Level – Answers
Winning Smiles

6b. Using evidence from the two articles and your own ideas, write an essay on the advantages and disadvantages of being beautiful.

20 - 16 Answers will contain a majority of these points:
- excellent use of evidence from the two articles, well chosen ideas that integrate with the argument
- the issue is discussed and views are expressed on both sides of the topic
- good planning with a clear structure, a progression of points and thoughtful conclusion
- technically very good, very few errors.

15 - 11 Answers will contain a majority of these points:
- good use of the articles although lacking the precision of the top band
- structure of the essay is likely to be more plodding, going through each point or argument for and against
- expression fair, not too repetitive
- own arguments are thoughtful but lack good examples
- technically sound although more obvious errors in punctuation and spelling.

10 - 6 Answers will contain a majority of these points:
- some use of the articles but a sense that the most apt points were missed
- own ideas are superficial and lack any evidence
- some sense of structure to the piece but, for example, the conclusion might be disappointing
- a working but limited vocabulary
- technically fair but noticeable errors throughout the piece.

5 or below Answers will contain a majority of these points:
- very little planning and a sense of jumping from point to point
- poorly selected pieces from the articles
- either overlong or not explained clearly
- many technical errors.

6c. A charity concerned with discrimination because of facial disfigurement has written a letter to a number of employers trying to educate them on the facts of this issue and urging them to change their attitude. Either write this letter or write the reply from one hotel chain that may not agree with the charity's arguments.

20 - 16 Answers will contain a majority of these points:
- appropriate letter layout, correct heading
- a carefully planned letter that develops its arguments
- each point is thoughtful and explained well
- some reference to the article or QED
- this piece may not be as long as the other two essay titles but it requires more subtlety in the tone of either letter
- technically very good.

15 - 11 Answers will contain a majority of these points:
- appropriate letter layout, correct heading
- a good letter but a more limited range of expression
- a good structure although points may not have been placed in their best order
- some reference to the article or QED
- technically good.

10 - 6 Answers will contain a majority of these points:
- appropriate letter layout, heading may not be correct such as an inappropriate address
- letter makes its points but in a heavyhanded way because the vocabulary is limited
- points unlikely to be supported by any examples other than opinion
- some technical errors throughout the piece.

5 or below Answers will contain a majority of these points:
- a letter layout but address is inappropriate if added at all
- a sense that the writer chose this title unwisely having few good points to make
- the tone of the letter is wrong
- many technical errors such as lack of paragraphing.

Guide to grade boundaries:	
41 - 37	A*
36 - 32	A
31 - 27	B
26 - 22	C
21 - 17	D
Below 17	U

Walk to school

Walk Talk
1.

The Pedestrians Association

On the one hand, CARS:

- Pollute the air we breathe.
- Cause acid rain and global warming.
- Use up vast amounts of energy and of the planet's limited natural resources.
- Harm the local environment.
- Create dangerous noise levels in our towns and cities.
- Kill or injure over 50,000 pedestrians in Britain every year.
- Are expensive to buy and to run.

On the other hand, WALKING:

- Does not pollute.
- Is environmentally friendly.
- Is healthy - walking four times a week for 30 minutes is very good for the heart. A brisk 20 minute walk every day will keep you fit.
- Improves the body's immune system.
- Relaxes you mentally.
- Cuts down on crime - areas where there are a lot of people walking about are not popular with criminals!
- Is not noisy.
- Is free.

Despite all this, fewer and fewer people are walking, and more and more are going by car. Why?

Well, it's mainly the result of a particularly vicious circle: the more people go by car, the worse conditions get for pedestrians. Then, because conditions for pedestrians are so bad, more people decide to go by car. And so it goes on...

Meanwhile, governments continue to spend ever increasing amounts of our money on roads in an attempt to make car journeys easier. As you probably know from experience, this money is largely spent in vain. Traffic jams and congestion, far from disappearing, are more common than ever. And all the time our air just keeps getting dirtier and our towns noisier and more unpleasant.

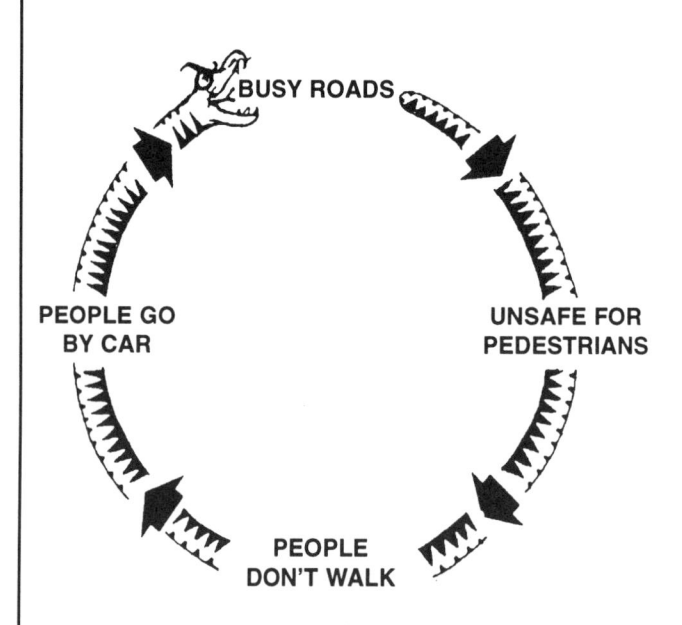

Steps to change

What is needed are some simple steps to replace the vicious circle with a kindly one. If we can make walking easier and safer, more people will leave the car at home. Walking will then become even easier and safer - and more people will leave the car at home. This will make us all healthier. It will dramatically improve the quality of life for everybody in the country.

THE VICIOUS CIRCLE

BUSY ROADS → UNSAFE FOR PEDESTRIANS → PEOPLE DON'T WALK → PEOPLE GO BY CAR → (back to BUSY ROADS)

Steps to change (cont)

How this can be done - and how you can help to get it done - will be revealed in Sections 4 to 8 of this pack. Before that, Sections 2 & 3 will explain in more detail just what a menace the car has become. Before that, though, a few words on the other major factor in the transport equation, namely...

Public Transport

Public transport produces much less pollution per person than private cars. It saves fuel, cuts down congestion and is a relatively cheap way for large numbers of people to travel. Look at these figures: (1)

- The average train journey costs 12p a mile
- The average bus journey costs 20p a mile.
- The average taxi journey costs £1.10 a mile.(2)
- The average cost of running a car is 34p a mile. (3)

You can see how much cheaper it is to travel by bus or train. You can also see why taxis (which are as environmentally harmful as cars in any case) are not the answer.

For the last few years our public transport system has been in decline. Fortunately, though, there have been hopeful signs recently. At last local and national governments seem to be realising that simply building new roads won't solve the problem of congestion. At last they seem to be realising that better public transport is essential. Think of the growing numbers of bus lanes in British towns or the reappearance of trams in places like Manchester.

The time has now come to look more closely at the car, and at the damage it causes. Fasten your seat belts for a rough ride....

(1) Figures from the Environmental Transport Association, based on costs in the early 90s.

(2) Less if more than one passenger

(3) Includes all fixed and running costs, and based on a car travelling 10,000 miles per year.

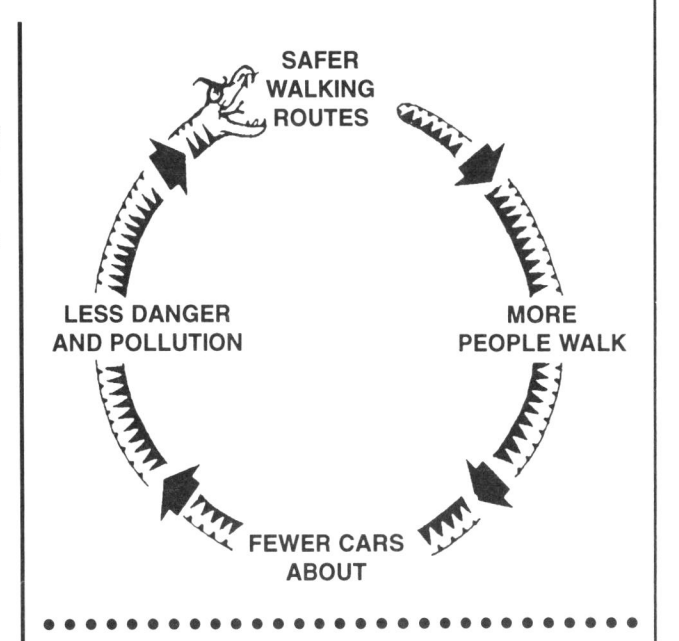

The Pedestrians Association 126 Aldersgate Street London EC1A 4JQ Tel: 0171 490 0750

Walk to school

AIR POLLUTION MONITORING RESULTS FROM BRECKNOCK PRIMARY SCHOOL, CLIFF VILLAS, LONDON BOROUGH OF CAMDEN

Introduction

In order to assess whether parents dropping their children off at school by car would cause levels of air pollution to rise, the Pollution Team carried out some carbon monoxide monitoring outside Brecknock primary school on 11 - 18 April 1996. Carbon monoxide monitors were put up on street lights opposite the school on 11 April and set to begin sampling. Data from the monitors was collected after one week. Carbon monoxide was considered to be the best pollutant to monitor because it comes almost entirely from petrol motor vehicles, so it is a good indicator of traffic pollution.

Results

The graph below shows that over one day during the term time, the levels of carbon monoxide rise quite considerably around 9.00 am which coincides with the beginning of classes at Brecknock School. This clearly shows that parents dropping their children off at school by car can have a significant impact on air quality. There does not appear to be a similar peak in the afternoon around 3.30 pm when parents pick their children up from school, which is probably due to the fact that in the afternoon wind speeds tend to be higher and pollution disperses more quickly. During the holiday period there is no carbon monoxide peak at 9.00 am showing that the air pollution during the term time is solely due to parents' car use, and is not due to normal rush hour traffic in that area.

Carbon monoxide levels at Brecknock Primary School 5.00am - 8.00pm

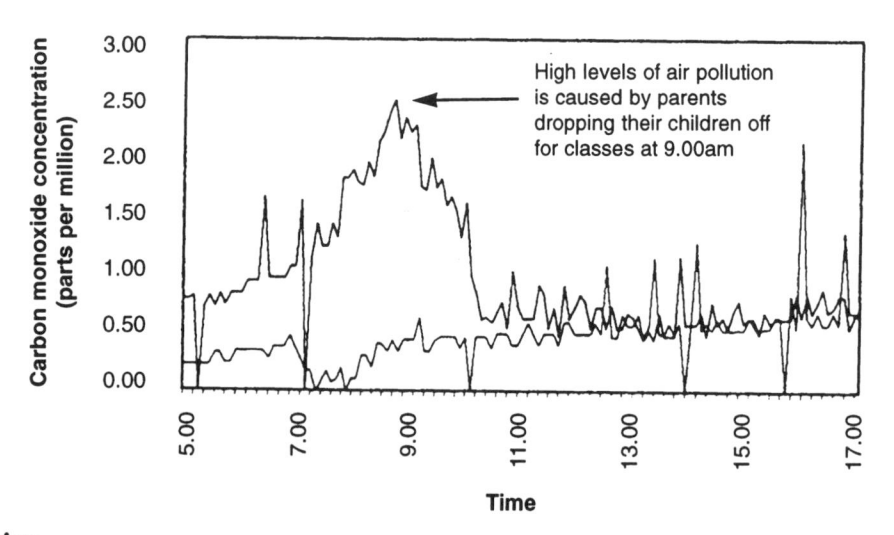

Conclusion

Short car journeys such as trips to school can adversely affect air quality by increasing the amount of air pollution in the surrounding area. If parents walked to school with their children, or took public transport, levels of air pollution would be reduced and there would be less congestion in the streets.

Walk to school

The Pedestrians Association 126 Aldersgate Street, London EC1A 4JQ
Tel. 0171 - 490 - 0750

WALKING TO SCHOOL: THE PARENT'S TALE

Moving house meant that Ann Henderson had to start walking her children to school as her husband needed the car. Let her experience speak for itself [1].

"I bought some comfortable shoes and resigned myself to walking.

The first thing that happened was the dead bird. Three year old Harry spotted it under a hedge. *"Why isn't it flying? Why is it dead? Can I pick it up?"* We decided it was best to leave it where it was, but the other questions had to be tackled as we walked along.

> Why should you and your children walk to school? Surely it will take longer, and in the winter won't the cold and rain be a real turn-off? Well, the health benefits of walking and the polluting effects of the car are well-known, but there are additional, surprising benefits too.

This early morning excursion into biology, philosophy and religion was something new. Formerly, as I negotiated parking restrictions, traffic lights and dodgy right turns, my conversation with the children had been of the sit-still-and-don't-fight variety.

The dead bird was probably only spottable by a short toddler on foot. Over the next few weeks we observed as it was gradually reduced to a few feathers. We observed other things too: the progress of growing things, including an unexpected and amazingly poisonous-looking toadstool; the progress of roadworks; the progress of traffic.

Traffic, of course, we now see from a very different viewpoint. It's more difficult to ignore the muck it creates when you watch your children inhaling it at pedestrian crossings.

The children's competitiveness developed too. One day the traffic was so bad that we gradually overtook on foot all the cars in which their friends were imprisoned.

The **Walk to school** campaign is part of the Pedestrians Association WALK 21 project. It is supported by the Department of the Environment's Environmental Action Fund and the Rees Jeffreys Road Fund. Charity No. 206006

Walk to school

It's much easier to teach road safety by doing it together. When the time comes to let them go out on foot alone I shall be much more confident than I would otherwise have been. Harry, in fact, now makes reproachful noises when anyone tries to cross the road without waiting for the green man.

I did wonder how we would feel about our new mode of transport once it got really cold. In fact I'm not sure it isn't more pleasant to walk in the cold than to sit in a cold car - by the time ours got warmed up we were already at school. What I do hate is the rain, and on those days I long for the car. But the children love it. They bounce about, splodging in puddles and shaking raindrops off overhanging branches.

Overall, the children's squabbling has reduced. The late afternoon used to be fairly dreadful, but an end-of-day walk, when we can compare notes on what we have done and talk through any problems at school, makes an excellent winding-down interlude and the children get home much more relaxed.

They also get home hungry. Instead of buying petrol, I'm buying food! Joanne used to be picky, but not now, and she is pinker and healthier looking too. And both of them sleep like logs, which they certainly didn't before.

My other fear had been over time but in fact I've almost gained time. As we close the door behind us and simply set off, with no hassles over keys and seat belts, it often feels quicker. I pick up whatever shopping I need on the way back, rather than making a separate journey later in the day.

But the clincher for me is the children themselves. As well as being fitter and happier, they know every inch of the routes we regularly cover, in the way I used to know every crack in the pavement when I was a child.

This intimate, child-level local knowledge makes them part of the neighbourhood. They recognise neighbours, trace the progress of a conker along a flooded gutter, watch the day-to-day development of a roof being repaired. And as we talk about it all, in a way we never seemed to have time for before, I get to know them better. I sometimes think I've lost a car and gained two children."

(1) Adapted from an article by Ann Henderson, first published in "Under Five Contact", the magazine of the Pre-School Learning Alliance, and subsequently in "Going Green", the magazine of the Environmental Transport Association.

Foundation Level – Questions

Walk to School

Time: _____

You will need to read both "AIR POLLUTION MONITORING RESULTS FROM BRECKNOCK PRIMARY SCHOOL, CLIFF VILLAS" and "WalkTalk 1" and answer the questions on both passages.

First read "Air Pollution Monitoring Results from Brecknock Primary School, Cliff Villas" and answer questions 1 to 7

1. What was the purpose of the monitoring? *(1 mark)*

2. Why did the school choose to monitor carbon monoxide in particular? *(1 mark)*

3. How are the afternoon results different from those for the morning? *(2 marks)*

4. What explanation is given for the difference between the morning and afternoon results? *(2 marks)*

5. The monitoring was carried out for one week. Why was a week chosen which included both term time and the school holiday? *(2 marks)*

6. How does the language and layout remind you of a science experiment? *(3 marks)*

7. In your own words, list the main points that are being made in the conclusion. *(4 marks)*

Now read "WalkTalk 1" and answer questions 8 to 10

8. List four different types of presentation used in this article. *(4 marks)*

9. Explain in your own words the "vicious circle" that results in less people walking. *(4 marks)*

10. What advantages does the writer claim that public transport has over private cars? *(4 marks)*

Walk to School   Foundation Level – Answers

Walk to School Marking Suggestions

Advised Time: 50 minutes

1. What was the purpose of the monitoring? *(1 mark)*
   - **check whether parents dropping children off at school causes levels of air pollution to rise.**

2. Why did the school choose to monitor carbon monoxide in particular? *(1 mark)*
   - **motor vehicles are the main source of carbon monoxide.**

3. How are the afternoon results different from those for the morning? *(2 marks)*
   - **a high level of carbon monoxide around 9am**
   - **no similar peak of carbon monoxide around 3.30pm.**

4. What explanation is given for the difference between the morning and afternoon results? *(2 marks)*
   - **windier in the afternoon than morning**
   - **the wind disperses the pollution.**

5. The monitoring was carried out for one week. Why was a week chosen which included both term time and the school holiday? *(2 marks)*
   - **for comparison**
   (1 mark with no explanation, but 2 marks if this is explained in terms of:)
   - **to find out whether the pollution is just caused by parents dropping off children at school.**

6. How does the language and layout remind you of a science experiment? *(3 marks)*
   1 mark each for 3 of:
   - **divided into separate sections each with its own heading**
   - **use of terms Introduction/Results/Conclusion for headings**
   - **use of graph**
   - **use of relatively formal language.**

7. In your own words, list the main points that are being made in the conclusion. *(4 marks)*
   (Any four points up to a maximum of four)
   - **short journeys by car can affect the air quality**
   - **it would be better if parents walked with their children to school**
   - **or went by bus or train**
   - **there would be less air pollution**
   - **and fewer traffic jams.**

"WalkTalk 1"

8. List four different types of presentation used in this article. *(4 marks)*
   - **tables of points listed (with bullet points)**
   - **"normal" text/prose/ordinary writing**
   - **diagrams to illustrate the vicious and kindly circles**
   - **cartoons showing the negative effects of cars and happy people in trains**
   the above points are the most probable but also allow:
   - **use of italics for footnotes.**

9. Explain in your own words the "vicious circle" that results in less people walking *(4 marks)*
   - **obviously the answer can start at any point on the circle**
   - **busy roads make conditions unsafe for pedestrians**
   - **because it is unsafe to walk, more people drive**
   - **when more people drive, the roads become busier, and so on.**
   Full marks for clear expression of all the points given here.
   No marks for merely copying out the relevant paragraph or diagram as the question stipulates, 'in your own words'.
   The two most important features needed for this answer are:
   a) *a method of showing how each point leads onto the next, so the wording of the answer requires some kind of link or 'bridge' between the points*
   b) *An indication that the process continues and feeds itself, such as 'and so on' at the end.*

10. What advantages does the writer claim that public transport has over private cars? *(4 marks)*
    - **costs less (per person, per mile)**
    - **pollutes less**
    - **saves fuel**
    - **reduces congestion.**

Higher Level – Questions

Walk to School

Time: _____

Additional questions for the HIGHER TIER candidates.
Read "Walking To School: the parent's tale"

1. How does the first paragraph suggest that at first Ann Henderson was not looking forward to walking her children to school?
   (1 mark)

2. What is the point of the writing inside the box between the two columns? Comment on the layout, purpose and the way language is used in this section.
   (4 marks)

3. In what ways and for what reasons were conversations different when Ann Henderson walked rather than drove her children to school?
   (5 marks)

4. Comment on the use of the word "progress" in the paragraph beginning "The dead bird ... "? How does the repeated use of this word reflect (or sum up) what the whole article is about?
   (4 marks)

5. Summarise the different benefits of walking to school described in the second page of this article.
   (8 marks)

Walk to School Marking Suggestions

Advised Time: 60 minutes

"Walking to school: the parent's tale"

1. How does the first paragraph suggest that at first Ann Henderson was not looking forward to walking her children to school? *(1 mark)*
   - **the word "resigned" suggests reluctance.**

2. What is the point of the writing inside the 'box' between the two columns? Comment on the layout, purpose and the way language is used in the box. *(4 marks)*
   Two marks for any combination of these points on layout and purpose:
   - *breaks up the article*
   - *makes it look more interesting/visual appeal*
   - *shading makes it stand out.*

   And two marks for any combination of these points on use of language:
   - *uses (rhetorical) questions to show the disadvantages of walking to increase the effect of giving the advantages*
   - *does not give all the advantages, only hints at them - and*
   - *tries to create interest/suspense to make reader want to read on by use of word "surprising".*

3. In what ways and for what reasons were conversations different when Ann Henderson walked rather than drove her children to school? *(5 marks)*
   (one for each point, up to five maximum)
   - *when driving, AH was tense because of the strain of driving*
   - *children were impatient/bored as they had no stimulation*
   - *so AH merely spoke to control children's behaviour*
   - *when walking, they encountered nature (and/or saw things not visible from the car)*
   - *more time to discuss what they saw*
   - *other changes followed, later it says they quarrel less and chat to neighbours.*

4. Comment on the use of the word "progress" in the paragraph beginning "the dead bird ..."? How does the repeated use of this word reflect (or sum up) what the whole article is about? *(4 marks)*
   One mark for noticing each of:
   - *at first used literally in relation to cycles of nature*
   - *then used in relation to roadworks, traffic congestion*

   Two further marks for delving deeper and noticing:
   - *emphasises that you see less interesting things driving rather than walking*
   - *the latter use is ironic / highlights negative aspects of driving*

5. Summarise the different benefits of walking to school described in the second page of this article. *(8 marks)*
   Any eight of the following:
   - *children gain better knowledge of road safety*
   - *cold weather less of a problem walking than in the car*
   - *allows children to wind down at the end of the school day and promotes better behaviour*
   - *health benefits: children eat better, sleep better, are fitter, healthier*
   - *saves money on petrol*
   - *easier to do shopping on way home, saves going out later*
   - *children's local knowledge increased*
   - *makes them part of the community*
   - *makes them more observant*
   - *improves relationship between mother and children.*

A guide to grade boundaries

The actual marks achieved for this paper are likely to differ from those for other papers in this book, as the tasks are somewhat different. Higher Tier candidates should achieve very high marks on the large number of relatively straightforward questions on the first two passages. They should, however, also be able to earn enough marks on the third passage to consolidate or improve their grade.

Strong Foundation candidates may also achieve high marks on the first two sections but are likely to find it harder to score highly on the third section.

To show how this may work numerically, there are 27 marks available in the first two passages which comprise the Foundation Tier, and a further 22 in the third passage, which, when added to the first two, comprises the Higher Tier.

Higher	
49 - 45	A*
44 - 40	A
39 - 35	B
34 - 30	C
29 - 25	D
24 or below	U

Foundation	
27 - 24	C
23 - 20	D
19 - 16	E
15 - 12	F
11 - 8	G
7 or below	U

Thus, candidates gaining C, the highest available grade on a Foundation Tier paper, by scoring, say, 25 marks out of 27 on the first two passages, need to score beween five and nine marks (out of 22) on the third passage to consolidate the C grade for the Higher Tier. If they score less than this, their mark would revert to a D.

To reach a B they would need to score at least 10 out of 22 on the third passage, (giving a total mark of 35,) and to reach an A, they would need to score at least 15 out of 22 on the third passage, (giving a total of 40.)

A candidate could obviously achieve a C grade on the Higher Tier while scoring less than 24 on the first two passages, but correspondingly more on the third passage. This may indicate definite Higher Tier potential but also the need to be more careful on relatively straightforward questions.

In general, the candidates' performance on the first two passages relative to the third, should provide an indication of their suitability for the Foundation or Higher Tier papers.

Woman with a winning punch who is barred from boxing

Kathy Marks

Jane Couch holds the women's world welterweight boxing title. She has fought at major events in America and in Europe, appearing on the same bill as some of the biggest names in men's boxing. But in her home country, she is effectively barred from professional competition.

The British Boxing Board of Control (BBBC), the sport's governing body, has always refused to license women, citing medical grounds. Without a licence, female professionals cannot compete at men's fights - the events that attract the promoters and the sponsorship money.

Couch, 28, has decided to provoke a showdown with the BBBC, which she accuses of being stuck in a chauvinistic time warp. Last week she applied for a licence, knowing she would be turned down. Now she plans to launch a court action, claiming restriction of trade and sexual discrimination. "It's ridiculous that I'm a world champion and I can't fight in Britain," said Couch, known as the "Fleetwood Assassin", after her Lancashire home town.

In the United States and in much of Europe, particularly France, Germany and Scandinavia, women's boxing is regarded as a legitimate sport and is followed avidly on television.

Some experts suggest that women are more vulnerable to head injuries than men, but others point out that they also throw a less-heavy punch. A recent meeting of the World Boxing Council's medical panel was told that the sport is no more dangerous for women than for men.

However, John Morris, general secretary of the BBBC, remains unconvinced. "There is the question of pregnancy, and of whether women should box during their... periods," he said. "Our doctors are ambivalent."

The board, which is taking legal advice on Couch's court action, has no plans to conduct any research on the subject. Mr Morris suggested that female professionals should set up their own licensing body.

"A lot of people on my board don't like the idea of women boxing and getting their faces knocked around," he said. "I may be old-fashioned, but neither do I. And just imagine the outcry if a woman got badly hurt."

Couch, naturally, scoffs at such sentiments, saying she has only ever suffered a few cuts and bruises - "nothing worse than you would get down the pub on a Saturday night". For her, the rush of adrenalin is the driving force. "I just love going into that ring," she said. She believes that her sport will eventually receive recognition in Britain and was heartened by the Amateur Boxing Association's decision last year to allow women and girls to fight. But for professionals, the only British events in which they can participate are all female fights, which are rarely staged because of scant interest from promoters and the shortage of high-calibre women.

Pauline Dickson, of the Association of Women Boxers, is circumspect. "You can't expect things to change overnight," she said. "But women's boxing is a hot potato that no one really wants to take responsibility for."

Couch, who started boxing two and a half years ago, won the world title last May in Copenhagen. She will defend it in August in Connecticut, on the same bill as Montell Griffin, the World Boxing Council light heavyweight champion.

But for the moment, her aggression is directed at the BBBC. "They've got a fight on their hands," she said.

The Independent
18 June 1997

Foundation Level – Questions

Woman with a winning punch

Time _____

Read the article "Woman with a winning punch who is barred from boxing" and answer the questions.

1. At which weight is Jane Couch a women's boxing world champion?
   (1 mark)

2. Why do women boxers want to fight at events where male boxers are also fighting? *(2 marks)*

3a. The British Boxing Board of Control refuses to give women a licence to box. What reasons are given in the article why women should not be allowed to box?
   (4 marks)

3b. Based on the article, how could you argue that women should be allowed to box?
   (6 marks)

4. Explain in your own words what the last paragraph means. *(2 marks)*

Choose one of the following questions:

5a. Write the newspaper report of Jane Couch's next fight. You can decide the result of the fight, but your report should show whether or not the newspaper takes women's boxing seriously. Set out your report like a newspaper article.
   (20 marks)

5b. A magazine for teenagers has invited its readers to send in their opinions on whether women should be allowed to box. Send in your own letter (or letters) on any aspect of this topic. You should write at least 200 words.
   (20 marks)

5c. Are there any jobs which can only be done by one of the sexes? Imagine this as a topic for a class debate and write a script giving the views of two or more pupils. Try to give detailed reasons and arguments rather than a long list of jobs.
   (20 marks)

Woman with a winning punch — Foundation Level – Answers

Woman with a winning punch Marking Suggestions   Advised time – 50 minutes.

1. At which weight is Jane Couch a women's boxing world champion? *(1 mark)*
   - welterweight

2. Why do women boxers want to fight at events where male boxers are also fighting? *(2 marks)*
   Either:
   - women want to compete in events where men are boxing because promoters and sponsors are more interested in men's events

   or
   - there is more money in these events.

3a. The British Boxing Board of Control refuses to give women a licence to box. What reasons are given in the article why women should not be allowed to box? *(4 marks)*

   The reasons given show signs of prejudice and lack of clear thinking, but it is not relevant to analyse them here; this should be saved for part b.
   One mark for each point, up to four:
   - women are more vulnerable to head injuries
   - women and pregnancy (the article does not specify whether the "danger" is to the women or their unborn children)
   - women and their periods (again the danger isn't specified)
   - male unease at women "getting their faces knocked around"
   - potential outcry if a woman was badly hurt.

3b. Based on the article, how could you argue that women should be allowed to box? *(6 marks)*

   The opposition to women fighting seems to be based on prejudice rather than facts/ it is old fashioned/ John Morris seems both vague and uncomfortable presenting his arguments (e.g. in relation to pregnancy and periods)/ it is chauvinistic.
   (This point is clearly important in the context of the article, and if expressed fully and well could earn most or even all of the available marks. Other points below are likely to be worth one mark, but up to two if fully argued.)
   - other countries allow it
   - medical evidence suggests it is no more dangerous for women than for men
   - specifically, the fact that women punch less hard than men nullifies the point about women and head injuries in 3a.

   above
   - Jane Couch points out that women fight in real life, ("down the pub") and boxing is no more dangerous than that
   - women can enjoy the adrenalin of getting into the ring to compete - either the competition itself or the danger.

4. Explain in your own words what the last paragraph means. *(2 marks)*
   Must show awareness of the use of a metaphor (though it isn't necessary to use the term metaphor.) i.e. She isn't literally going to fight anyone, but is taking legal action against the BBBC to force them to license her.

The mark scheme for Question 5 applies to both tiers but note that question 5b differs slightly between the tiers:

5a. Write the newspaper report of Jane Couch's next fight. You can decide the result of the fight, but your report should show whether or not the newspaper takes women's boxing seriously. Set out your report like a newspaper article. *(20 marks)*

   20-16 Answers will contain a majority of these points
   - the layout should accurately conform to a newspaper layout
   - the language used should contain significant elements of newspaper language and should be consistent either as tabloid or broadsheet
   - the attitude towards women's boxing should be consistent and clear, whether it is serious or frivolous and supports or is opposed to women's boxing
   - technically very good at the top end with few errors.

   15 – 11 Answers will contain a majority of these points
   - the layout should conform in most respects to a newspaper layout
   - the language used should contain elements of newspaper language and should be broadly consistent either as tabloid or broadsheet
   - there should be a discernible and broadly consistent attitude towards women's boxing, whether the attitude is serious or

frivolous, and supports or is opposed to women's boxing
- *technically fair but there may be common and repeated errors.*

Penalise mis-spellings of words that are in the article

10 – 6 Answers will contain a majority of these points:
- *the layout should show some effort to conform to a newspaper layout*
- *the language used should contain elements of newspaper language*
- *there should be some elements of an attitude towards women's boxing, whether the attitude is serious or frivolous, and supports or is opposed to it*
- *technically weak but not hindering comprehension.*

5 or less Answers will contain a majority of these points:
- *the layout is unlikely to conform successfully to a newspaper layout*
- *the language will show few if any elements of newspaper language*
- *the report may simply describe a fight and show few if any elements of an attitude towards women's boxing, whether serious or frivolous, and supportive or opposed to women's boxing*
- *technically weak*

5b. (Foundation Level) A magazine for teenagers has invited its readers to send in their opinions on whether women should be allowed to box. Send in your own letter (or letters) on any aspect of this topic. You should write at least 200 words   (20 marks)

5b. (Higher Level) A magazine for teenagers has invited its readers to send in their opinions on whether women should be allowed to box. Send in two (or more) letters on any aspect of this topic giving different points of view.
(20 marks)

20-16 Answers will contain a majority of these points:
- *appropriate format for letters to a magazine*
- *an appropriate personal tone and use of persuasive language*
- *if more than one letter is attempted, then a clear contrast of views and in the best candidates, even of style and linguistic features between the different letters*
- *if one letter is written, then the points raised should be given in some depth, especially if they are ones that were raised in the article*
- *technically very good at the top end with few errors.*

15-11 Answers will contain a majority of these points:
- *an awareness in the format that the task involves letters to a magazine*
- *some attempt at an appropriate personal tone and use of persuasive language*
- *if more than one letter is attempted, then some contrast in the views and in the language between the different letters*
- *if one letter is written, then the points raised should have enough depth to avoid reading like a list of points raised in the article*
- *technically fair but there may be common and repeated errors.*

Penalise mis-spellings of words that are in the article

10-6 Answers will contain a majority of these points:
- *an awareness in the format that the task involves letters*
- *some attempt at an appropriate personal tone and use of persuasive language*
- *if more than one letter is attempted the contrast in the views is likely to be very basic and little contrast in the language between the different letters is likely - if one letter is written, then the points raised may not have enough depth to avoid reading like a list of points raised in the article*
- *technically weak but not hindering comprehension.*

5 or less Answers will contain a majority of these points:
- *little account taken in the format or the language that the task involves writing a letter/letters to a magazine*
- *little argument based on the issues raised in the article*
- *possible unassimilated material reproduced inappropriately*
- *technically weak.*

Woman with a winning punch — Foundation Level – Answers

5c. Are there any jobs which can only be done by one of the sexes? Imagine this as a topic for a class debate and write a script giving the views of two or more pupils. Try to give detailed reasons and arguments rather than a long list of jobs. *(20 marks)*

The wording of the question allows for different formats. It uses the word "script" but of a debate, so two (or more) longish speeches or a dialogue involving an exchange of views would both be acceptable.

20 – 16 Answers will contain a majority of these points:
- *a clear attempt to use persuasive language*
- *the presence of at least two differing views*
- *a logical deployment of argument avoiding repetition or mere assertion*
- *technically very good at the top end with few errors.*

15 – 11 Answers will contain a majority of these points:
- *some attempt to use persuasive language*
- *the presence of differing views, but increasingly likely to be only two views towards the lower end of this grade*
- *avoidance of a list, but there may be difficulty in sustaining a logical argument towards the lower end of this scale*
- *technically fair but there may be common and repeated errors.*

Penalise mis-spellings of words that are in the article.

10 – 6 Answers will contain a majority of these points:
- *the language will increasingly be in the pupil's own voice towards the lower end of this scale*
- *probably evidence of different views*
- *the speeches will have some structure but will tend towards mere assertion and may involve prejudice rather than argument*
- *technically weak but not hindering comprehension.*

5 or less Answers will contain a majority of these points:
- *no attempt at a voice other than the pupil's own*
- *little or no evidence of more than one point of view*
- *little or no sense of structure in the presentation of points*
- *a tendency to list jobs and use prejudice rather than argument*
- *technically weak.*

Guide to grade boundaries	
35 - 30	C
29 - 24	D
23 - 18	E
17 - 12	F
11 - 8	G
Below 8	U

Higher Level – Questions
Woman with a winning punch

Time: _____

Read the article "Woman with a winning punch who is barred from boxing" and answer the questions.

1. From the first paragraph explain how Jane Couch is treated differently in Britain and abroad. *(2 marks)*

2. To what extent can you separate facts from opinions in the article in relation to the safety of women's boxing? Use examples in your answer. *(4 marks)*

3. What evidence is there in the passage that John Morris is not very comfortable talking about this issue? *(4 marks)*

4. What impression do you get of Jane Couch's personality from this article? *(8 marks)*

Choose one of the following questions:

5a. Write the newspaper report of Jane Couch's next fight. You can decide the result of the fight, but your report should show whether or not the newspaper takes women's boxing seriously. Set out your report like a newspaper article. *(20 marks)*

5b. A magazine for teenagers has invited its readers to send in their opinions on whether women should be allowed to box. Send in two (or more) letters on any aspect of this topic giving different points of view. *(20 marks)*

5c. Are there any jobs which can only be done by one of the sexes? Imagine this as a topic for a class debate and write a script giving the views of two or more pupils. Try to give detailed reasons and arguments rather than a long list of jobs. *(20 marks)*

Woman with a winning punch Marking Suggestions   Advised time – 50 minutes.

1. From the first paragraph explain how Jane Couch is treated differently in Britain and abroad. *(2 marks)*
   Include the first point and either/both of the next two
   - is not able to fight in Britain
   - can fight in America and Europe
   - can fight on the same bill as male boxers.

2. To what extent can you separate facts from opinions in the article in relation to the safety of women's boxing? *(4 marks)*
   This is complex, both in itself and in avoiding repeating information needed for other questions.
   A simpler version of this question could have asked students to give examples of facts, opinions and statements which might be either. Even though the question does not require this approach, it would be a sensible one to adopt as it allows specific points to be made which are likely to be rewarded with marks. A more reflective, less mechanical answer could still earn full marks.
   The answer should reflect the difficulty of separating fact and opinion in the article, with at least two marks for any of the points below:
   - the differences in the situation women boxers face in different countries is a fact referred to in question 1. It would be an opinion to claim that the differing regulations reflect different views of safety issues (as opposed, say, to being based on questions of equality)
   - phrases like "some experts suggest" are dressed up to sound like facts, but the only fact seems to be that the experts differ, so it would be reasonable to regard all the medical points in the article as opinion in the sense that they are not proven
   - John Morris refers to pregnancy and periods and it is a fact that only women and not men become pregnant and have periods. But he produces no safety evidence in relation to pregnancy and periods, so they cannot be regarded as facts in terms of the argument
   - his later references to attitudes to women fighting and getting hurt are clearly opinions
   - Jane Couch's comments also seem to be opinions, although she could claim that they are based on the facts of her own experience (adrenalin rushes and fights in pubs on a Saturday night.)

3. What evidence is there in the passage that John Morris is not very comfortable talking about this issue? *(4 marks)*
   Up to two marks for each of the following points if well expressed:
   - *John Morris raises the question of pregnancy, but then says nothing more about it. He obviously could have said that there would be a danger to unborn children if women unknowingly fought in the early stages of pregnancy. The fact that he didn't say this suggests that he may have been too embarrassed*
   - this impression is reinforced by the ellipsis before the word "periods" which suggests an embarrassed pause
   - he knows that he may be accused of being "old fashioned" because he objects to women "getting their faces knocked around".

4. What impression do you get of Jane Couch's personality from this article? *(8 marks)*
   - aggressive for taking on the British Board of Control in a legal action, for her comments about fighting in pubs on a Saturday night, for her comments about loving to get in the ring, and the rush of adrenalin, for her final comment about the BBBC having a fight on their hands
   - prepared to stick up for her rights and the rights of women
   - she regards the BBBC's position as being chauvinistic, and won't stand for it
   - intelligent/cunning in terms of her tactics in applying for a licence, knowing she would be turned down, in order to provide the grounds for launching a court case
   One or two marks for each of the above points depending on quality of expression and for pointing out that she seems to combine several different qualities.

For Question 5 see page 86.

Guide to grade boundaries	
38 - 36	A*
35 - 32	A
31 - 28	B
27 - 24	C
23 - 19	D
18 or below	U

Can Teletubbies really be good for young children?

By TONY HALPIN
Education Correspondent

ONE sings in Cantonese, the others often burble incomprehensibly, and they all have a tendency to dance around a lot.

But what the Teletubbies barely seem able to do is speak English, which has many parents wondering exactly what the BBC's latest educational programme is teaching their children.

Unlike in the good old days of Play School, no one looks through the round window in this world. Instead the four brightly-coloured creatures point to televisions in their stomachs showing films of children taking part in different activities.

The 'goo goo' speaking style of the Teletubbies – Tinky Winky, Dipsy, Laa Laa and Po – has caused a backlash among parents.

Some have complained to the BBC that the meaningless baby-talk is a poor substitute for the songs and stories in the long-running Playdays, which Teletubbies has replaced in the morning slot.

'Talking' Teletubbies - but they don't speak English

The programme's creators insist the series reflects the technological times in which

'A series which reflects the times'

'nobody talks to babies' any more and where children are increasingly 'coming to school without words'.

They argue that the series is 'child-centred', encouraging youngsters aged two to five to learn by playing along with the characters. Teletubbies is the most expensive pre-school series in the BBC's history. The corporation has already commissioned 250 25-minute episodes over the next three years from the independent production company, Ragtime.

Filmed in Teletubbyland – actually a grassy hill in Warwickshire – the creatures live with rabbits and 'voice trumpets', which look like submarine periscopes and pop out of the ground to make announcements from the 'real world'.

They exist on a diet of custard and toast and share their 'Tubbytronic Superdrome' home with a vacuum cleaner called Noo Noo.

The four Teletubbies, who are portrayed by actors in costumes, have been described as looking like 'big babies weighed down by their nappies'.

Po, coloured red, is the smallest Teletubby and is

Teletubbies

'highly excitable'. Her special song means 'quick, quick, quick' or 'slow, slow, slow' in Cantonese though children never actually learn this from the show.

Laa Laa is yellow and described as 'the happiest, smiliest – and second-smallest of the Teletubbies'. Her favourite word is 'nice'.

Dipsy is the second-largest, and green. He 'sets himself apart a bit as he tries to be cool'. Words to his special song are 'bptum, bptum, bptum, bptum'.

Tinky Winky, purple, is the 'largest and gentlest' Teletubby who 'loves to dance and fall over'. His song goes 'Tinky winky biddle biddle boddle'.

Writer and co-creator Andrew Davenport said Teletubbies had been tested on seven 'focus groups' of children and parents across the country.

He insisted the programme was in the tradition of classics such as Watch With Mother and the Flowerpot Men. But he conceded the shows were aimed towards the youngest children in the age range. 'They are purposely pitched at a lower age level so that the children are given the feeling that they know slightly more than the Tubbies because the Tubbies know nothing,' he said. A BBC spokesman admitted there had been 'a fair few' complaints from parents. One mother, Sarah Spicer, said her three-year-old son Steffan had been an avid viewer of Playdays but was so unimpressed by Teletubbies that he did not watch it after the first episode. Mrs Spicer, Llandyssul, Cardiganshire, said: 'There is too much "goo goo" and dancing around doing meaningless things, whereas in Playdays there were interesting stories and ideas which you could follow through and talk about.' Anne Wood – Teletubbies' creative director, dismissed the complaints, saying 'There has been some articulate criticism from a narrow band of people who have pre-conceived ideas of what education is. 'We are not a school, we are an entertainment programme for young children. We have a responsibility to treat our audience with respect.'

How story-telling reached the end

GENERATIONS of children grew up learning to 'look through the round window' and other story-telling entrances in Play School, which ran from 1964 to 1988.

It was replaced by Playbus and then Playdays. Repeats of Playdays are now being shown in the afternoons but there are no plans for any new series.

A variety of children's shows down the years have featured characters which did not speak English.

Children delighted in the 'Flobbadob' speech of Bill and Ben the flowerpot men, the strange whistling noises of the Clangers, and the squeaky voice of Sooty's friend Sweep.

Sooty's voice was never heard although his thoughts were relayed by his creator, Harry Corbett, later replaced by his son Matthew.

Another pre-school hero who remained silent was Andy Pandy.

Daily Mail, May 20 1997

Letters

Tubbies or no tubbies: that is the question

I WAS SHOCKED to discover that one of my 3½ year old son's favourite programmes was to be taken off in favour of the new programme *Teletubbies*, supposedly suitable for ten-month to five-year-old children. Having seen the first few editions, neither I nor my son was impressed.

"Nobody talks to babies . . . so, increasingly, children are coming to school without words," stated *Teletubbies* creator Anne Wood in RT (29 March - 4 April). So what have we replaced the storytelling and clear explanations of Playdays with? The "goo-goo" style narrative of *Teletubbies* together with films of children in potentially interesting situations, but with little or no explanation. My son, Steffan, kept asking, "What are they doing, why are they doing that?" I would disagree with Ms Woods that children of my son's age would benefit from watching this show on their own. Steffan just gave up and walked away, saying he wanted Whybird back.

I agree that *Teletubbies* might be suitable for children of two years and under, but this now leaves a big hole for the two- to five-year-olds. The *Playdays* repeats are shown at a time when many parents are collecting older children from school, and may be missed by their younger siblings.

Sarah Spicer
Llandysul, Cardiganshire

. . . WOULD YOU PLEASE give me the telephone number of a counselling service for toddlers who are suffering from "cold turkey" due to the sudden removal of *Playdays*?

Who on earth thought it would be a good idea to deprive the nation's toddlers of the friends they have seen every day for their whole lives and replace them with weird alien creatures that 'can't even talk properly' (my four-year-old son Matthew's words, not mine)?

I think there is a case for *Rough Justice* here – Free the *Playdays* Three!

Michelle Jones
Waterlooville, Hampshire

. . . ONCE UPON A TIME, there was a mummy and three children who loved *Playdays*. Then the Wicked Witch from the Bad Baron's Castle took their favourite programme away. The children asked where their friends had gone. The Wicked Witch said, "You must watch my new programme instead. When you do, you'll fall asleep for 25 minutes and your mother will wish she was a frog." The children asked how they could break the spell. "You can't," said the Wicked Witch, "because I am never wrong." The children sighed and went to play in the garden instead.

Liz Duffy
Royston, Hertfordshire

.... AT LAST, A children's programme that my toddler will watch, so Mum can put her feet up and we can all watch these loveable, cuddly creatures. I'd like to say a big thank you to the BBC for *Teletubbies*. It's entertaining, it's fun, it's educational and it has saved me from endless repeats of *Top Gear Motorsport* (my little girl's previous favourite viewing).

Helen McNeill
Dornoch, Sutherland

Radio Times, May 1997

Teletubbies   *Foundation Level – Questions*

Time: _____

Read 'Can Teletubbies really be good for young children?' and 'How story-telling reached the end' and then answer the questions.

1. From the first five paragraphs of the main article, 'Can Teletubbies really be good for young children?', list five different ways the Teletubbies speak, as described by the author. *(5 marks)*

2. Which children's programme does the writer approve of? Support your example with one quotation from the articles. *(2 marks)*

3. Using the main article, apart from the way the Teletubbies look and speak, list three other unusual facts about them. *(3 marks)*

4. From paragraphs 6 and 7 of 'Can Teletubbies really be good for young children?', list two ways in which the programme makers defend the language of the Teletubbies. *(2 marks)*

5. Is Teletubbies the first children's programme not to use proper English? Support your answer with some evidence from both 'Can Teletubbies really be good for young children?' and 'How story-telling reached the end'. *(2 marks)*

6. Give one fact to show the BBC's confidence in the programme. *(1 mark)*

7. Do you think the article's main headline is for or against the programme? Explain your decision. *(2 marks)*

Answer one of the questions below:
Use your own experience and the information you have found in the two news articles.

8a. The BBC has asked you to submit your plans for a new programme for 3-5 year olds. Write at least 200 words that describe your new programme and also explain how it will satisfy children and their parents. *(20 marks)*

8b. Anne Wood, the Producer of Teletubbies says, ' We are not a school, we are an entertainment programme for young children.' Do you think her view is right? Should children's television educate or entertain? *(20 marks)*

8c. Imagine you are in charge of children's television. There have been a lot of complaints in the Radio Times recently that children's programmes do not help to educate young people. They have also said that there are too many cartoons, Australian soaps and too much drama that shows bad behaviour. Write an article for the Radio Times that defends some of the programmes that are shown. Use actual examples of programmes to help your argument. *(20 marks)*

Foundation Level – Answers

Teletubbies

Teletubbies Marking Suggestions

Advised time – 60 / 75 minutes.

1. From the first five paragraphs of the main article, 'Can Teletubbies really be good for young children?' list five different ways the Teletubbies speak as described by the author. *(5 marks)*
   - one sings in Cantonese
   - others burble incomprehensibly
   - they barely speak English
   - meaningless baby talk
   - goo-goo speaking style

2. Which children's programme does the writer approve of? Support your example with one quotation from the articles. *(2 marks)*
   - approval of Play School
   - 'unlike in the good old days of Play School' or 'generations of children grew up learning to look through the round window'.

3. Using the main article, apart from the way the Teletubbies look and speak, list three other unusual facts about them. *(3 marks)*

   Any three:
   - they live with rabbits
   - they live with voice trumpets
   - they exist on a diet of custard and toast
   - they live with a vacuum cleaner called Noo Noo.
   - they live in Teletubby land
   - they live in a Tubbytronic Superdrome.

4. From paragraphs 6 and 7 of 'Can Teletubbies really be good for young children?', list two ways in which the programme makers defend the language of the Teletubbies. *(2 marks)*
   - it reflects the technical times, nobody talks to babies
   - increasingly children are coming to school without words

   Note: Only award points about Language as requested.

5. Is Teletubbies the first children's programme not to use proper English? Support your answer with some evidence from both 'Can Teletubbies really be good for young children?' and 'How story-telling reached the end'. *(2 marks)*
   - other children's programmes have not used proper English
   - many examples in the accompanying feature such as Bill and Ben, Clangers, Sooty.

6. Give one fact to show the BBC's confidence in the programme. *(1 mark)*
   - The corporation has already commissioned 250 episodes.

7. Do you think the article's main headline is for or against the programme? Explain your decision. *(2 marks)*
   - the implication is that the writer is not impressed (against) the programme
   - the headline is questioning the reader underlining '*really*', suggests that the programme cannot, in fact, be good for children.

Guide to grade boundaries Foundation level Questions 1 - 7	
17 - 16	C
15 - 14	D
13 - 12	E
11 - 10	F
9 - 8	G
Below 8	U

Question 8 Answer scheme: Note to the teacher: Because question 8 is common to both levels, this answer scheme is suitable for the Foundation and Higher students. The Foundation students can 'officially' earn a maximum of 20 marks taking them to a mid-C grade. If you offer over 20 marks to Foundation students, even if their work for this question is very good, then it may skew their overall result. Higher candidates can earn up to 30 marks. The suggested grade boundaries are beside the marks.

8a. The BBC has asked you to submit your plans for a new programme for 3-5 year olds. Describe your new programme and also explain how it will satisfy children and their parents.

Note: Students are likely to draw on their own experience and viewing and their ideas may be slight variations on existing programmes. Do not penalise students too much for this but consider the quality of expression and presentation of ideas.

30 – 25 (Approximately grades A* to B) Answers will contain a majority of these points:
- *a detailed and developed answer, the student has thought about how to plan and present their answer with about one third devoted to justifying the type of programme*
- *the brief has been closely followed, the target audience identified which is both parents and children*
- *the student has a good understanding of what might interest a young child and incorporated these ideas into a suitable*

Teletubbies
Foundation Level – Answers

     programme format
- *the ideas are not too derivative of current or previous programmes*
- *a sense that they are describing a serial as requested, not just one programme*
- *a wide range of expression which explains the programme idea clearly*
- *technically excellent with confident use of punctuation and few or no spelling errors.*

24 – 19 (Approximately grades B- to D) Answers will contain a majority of these points:
- *a planned answer with a sense of structure so that the programme's contents are in some sort of order and with explanations about the content*
- *both aspects of the brief are covered but there may be slightly too much given to one of the two*
- *the ideas are suitable but the student may not have realised the potential of the ideas*
- *expression is good although there may be a tendency to repetition and a more limited vocabulary in the lower part of this mark band*
- *technically fair. The work is paragraphed. There may be errors though in punctuation and some spellings of more complex words.*

18 – 13 (Approximately grades D- to F+) Answers will contain a majority of these points:
- *an awareness of both aspects of the question although justification of the ideas may be brief and superficial*
- *a simple idea for a programme and not the foresight to see how it could be developed*
- *expression is fair at the top end of this band but ideas may be expressed simply and there may be a tendency to repeat phrases or use generalisations*
- *technically fair in places but errors in paragraphing, some sentence structure and spellings. Be severe on mis-spellings of words that are in the resource material.*

12 – 7 (Approximately grades F to G) Answers will contain a majority of these points:
- *an answer that may not cover both aspects of the question*
- *too much time may have been devoted to one aspect of the programme rather than considering the whole programme*
- *an idea that is highly derivative, perhaps just variations on existing names like Terry The Tank Engine*
- *few, if any, ideas on how the series might develop*
- *weak expression which may confuse the reader*
- *frequent errors in punctuation and spellings.*

8b. Anne Wood, the Producer of Teletubbies says, 'We are not a school, we are an entertainment programme for young children.' Do you think her view is right? Should children's television educate or entertain?

30 – 25 (Approximately grades A* to B) Answers will contain a majority of these points:
- *a well-organised essay that shows a progression of ideas as they argue their points*
- *a well-structured essay that includes a good opening and conclusion*
- *reference to the article and to other television programmes to support their views, these could include ones from the smaller news article*
- *the argument does not have to be balanced but there should be consideration from both angles, e.g. the comments about language skills from the programme makers and the counter-arguments from the newspaper and the viewers' letters*
- *expression is confident with few, if any, technical errors at the top of this band*

24 – 19 (Approximately grades B- to D) Answers will contain a majority of these points:
- *an organised essay although points may not have been presented in the best order*
- *an answer that keeps to the set question*
- *less balance to the argument, consideration of one of the two aspects may be superficial*
- *reference to the articles or other television programmes to support their views*
- *good expression but vocabulary is more limited than top band work*
- *a more limited range of punctuation and some spelling errors*

18 - 13 (Approximately grades D- to F+) Answers will contain a majority of these points:
- *some organisation but points are likely to be presented as they occurred to the writer*
- *little development of ideas and few, if any, examples to support opinions*
- *an unbalanced argument that may not consider both aspects of the question*
- *the essay may stray from the question set or repeat points because of lack of ideas*
- *fair but repetitive expression*
- *noticeable errors in punctuation and spelling.*

12 – 7 (Approximately grades F to G) Answers will contain a majority of these points:

- an unorganised approach where points may not relate or be repeated
- uncertainty of what is required for the essay, some of the content may be irrelevant
- little or no reference to the article and other programmes or
- too much on a particular programme without drawing conclusions from the example
- unoriginal thinking and opinionated views
- expression is poor, ideas are not paragraphed
- many errors in spelling and punctuation.

8c. Imagine you are in charge of children's television. There have been a lot of complaints in the Radio Times recently that children's programmes do not help to educate young people. They have also said that there are too many cartoons, Australian soaps and too much drama that shows bad behaviour. Write an article for the Radio Times that defends some of the programmes that are shown. Use actual examples of programmes to help your argument.

30 – 25 (Approximately grades A* to B) Answers will contain a majority of these points:
- well-organised work that shows a progression of ideas as they argue their points
- a well structured article that includes a good opening and a thoughtful conclusion for the reader
- reference to programmes, as requested, but conclusions are explained from each example, rather than expecting the reader to draw their own conclusion
- an understanding of why there may have been complaints but a good defence of the BBC's children's programmes
- possible arguments might be the cultural diversity of foreign soaps, the need for light relief after a hard school day, morally challenging material that doesn't patronise its viewers
- a suitable style for the piece. At the top end the writing will have style and pace and sound like a magazine article, not an English essay
- technically excellent with confident use of punctuation and few or no spelling errors.

24 – 19 (Approximately grades B- to D) Answers will contain a majority of these points:
- an organised piece although points may not be presented in their best order
- in the lower part of this band there may be a tendency to list 'good' programmes without explaining their merit
- a fair defence of the programmes but some justification may be superficial or brief e.g.

'a good programme is Grange Hill because it is about real life issues', but the issues are not mentioned or the matter explored further
- a sense of the piece being an article, not merely an English essay, such as informal expression and rhetorical questions
- good expression but vocabulary is more limited than top band work
- technically fair. The work is paragraphed. There may be errors though in punctuation and some spellings of more complex words.

18 – 13 (Approximately grades D- to F) Answers will contain a majority of these points:
- some organisation but points are likely to be presented as they occurred to the writer
- examples are used but there is little explanation of why they have been chosen
- they may make the same points over again not progressing the argument
- the piece is not likely to read much like a magazine article
- expression is fair at the top end of this band but ideas may be expressed simply and there may be a tendency to repeat phrases or use generalisations
- technically fair in places but errors in paragraphing, some sentence structure and spellings.

12 – 7 (Approximately grades F to G)
- an unorganised piece that frequently returns to the same points
- few examples may be used to defend their viewpoint or
- numerous examples, such as a long list of programmes with a superficial comment on why they are 'good'
- there may be some confusion on what is required for the article and so they stray off the point
- expression is limited which may confuse the reader
- frequent errors in punctuation and spelling.

Teletubbies *Higher Level – Questions*

Time: _____

Read both newspaper articles 'Can Teletubbies really be good for young children?' and 'How storytelling reached the end' and the Letters section from the Radio Times and then answer the questions.

1. From the first five paragraphs of the main article, 'Can Teletubbies really be good for young children?' list five different ways the Teletubbies speak, as described by the author.   *(5 marks)*

2. Give one fact to show the BBC's confidence in the programme.   *(1 mark)*

3. In 'Can Teletubbies really be good for young children' a BBC spokesman admitted that 'there have been a fair few complaints'. What is he really saying? *(2 marks)*

4. From the main news article, 'Can Teletubbies really be good for young children?', what contradictions are there concerning the intended age range for Teletubbies? *(2 marks)*

5. Look at Liz Duffy's letter. Summarise the main points she is making to the BBC. *(5 marks)*

6. What is the main complaint of the letters page and the main complaint of the article?   *(2 marks)*

7. Using only the presentation in the two news articles (not the letters) is there a positive or negative bias towards Teletubbies? Give three examples to justify your opinion.   *(6 marks)*

Answer one of the questions below:

8a. The BBC has asked you to submit your plans for a new programme for 3-5 year olds. Describe your new programme and also explain how it will satisfy children and their parents.   *(30 marks)*

8b. Anne Wood, the Producer of Teletubbies says, ' We are not a school, we are an entertainment programme for young children.' Do you think her view is right? Should children's television educate or entertain?   *(30 marks)*

8c. Imagine you are in charge of children's television. There have been a lot of complaints in the Radio Times recently that children's programmes do not help to educate young people. They have also said that there are too many cartoons, Australian soaps and too much drama that shows bad behaviour. Write an article for the Radio Times that defends some of the programmes that are shown. Use actual examples of programmes to help your argument.   *(30 marks)*

Teletubbies Marking Suggestions

Advised time – 75 minutes.

Reminder: The Higher Level covers the same material as the Foundation level with additional reading and more demanding questions on style in the first section. The second sections are almost identical but require a higher level of expression and development.
This exercise may be useful for assessing students who sit on the borderline of the two examinations.

1. From the first five paragraphs of the main article, 'Can Teletubbies really be good for young children?', list five different ways Teletubbies speak as described by the author. *(5 marks)*
   - *one sings in Cantonese*
   - *others burble incomprehensibly*
   - *they barely speak English*
   - *meaningless baby talk*
   - *goo-goo speaking style.*

2. Give one fact to show the BBC's confidence in the programme. *(1 mark)*
   - *the corporation has already commissioned 250 episodes.*

3. In 'Can Teletubbies really be good for young children?', a BBC spokesman admitted that 'there have been a fair few complaints'. What is he really saying? *(2 marks)*
   - *'admitted' so the answer was not given readily*
   - *'fair few' is a euphemism for quite a lot of complaints!*
   Note: Both these points may be given in one sentence.

4. From the main news article, 'Can Teletubbies really be good for young children?', what contradictions are there concerning the intended age range for Teletubbies? *(2 marks)*
   - *'the programme's creators insist … the series is child-centred encouraging youngsters aged two to five'*
   - *'writer and co-creator .. conceded the shows were aimed towards the youngest children in the age range'.*

5. Look at Liz Duffy's letter. Summarise the main points she is making to the BBC. *(5 marks)*
   - *she and her children loved Playdays*
   - *the BBC has taken Playdays off*
   - *the new programme is dull and uninteresting*
   - *the BBC won't change their mind and take it off*
   - *her children have stopped watching television.*

6. What is the main complaint of the letters page and the main complaint of the article? *(2 marks)*
   - *the letters page complains about the loss of Playdays*
   - *the news article's complaint is about the language used in Teletubbies.*

7. Using only the presentation in the two news articles (not the letters) is there a positive or negative bias towards Teletubbies? Give three examples to justify your opinion. *(6 marks)*
   One mark for the example and one mark for explaining it, if only briefly.
   - *really underlined in the headline, asking you to question it again, implying that it probably isn't good for children*
   - *the main picture caption, 'but they don't speak English' suggests they are not, therefore, teaching children to speak it.*
   - *the second article's headline, How story-telling reached the end. Seen as the loss of a worthy skill.*

Guide to grade boundaries Higher level Questions 1 - 7	
23 - 22	A*
21 - 19	A
18 - 16	B
15 - 13	C
12 - 10	D
Below 10	U

See pages 95 - 97 for answers and grade boundaries for question 8.

Teletubbies – Sample Essay 1

Anne Wood says, 'We are not a school, we are an entertainment programme for young children.' Do you think her view is right? Should children's television educate or entertain?

We are not a school, we are a entertainment programe for young children says Ann Wood. She is talking about teletubbies which is a programme which is on the BBC for young children. Its on twice a day. I have a younger brother aged eight and he watches it and so does my sister whose four and she thinks its great. She has lots of Teletubbies posters in her room and she has two of the Teletubby dolls which she dresses up and which are very specal to her. If theres a picture in a magazine of the Teletubbies she will cut it out because she collects anything to do with Teletubbies. Sometimes I watch Teletubbies and I think its alright. My brother won't cut out pictures from magazines as he's older.

Their have been a lot of complaints about Teletubbies and people have said that 'nobody talks to babies anymore' and children 'are increasingly coming to school without words.'

Their have been a lot of complaints that the Teletubbies don't speak proper English but speak in Cantonese. I don't think this is bad as long as the children are spoken to in English so the parents explain what is going on. In one programme I saw they told a story in English so some English is used in the program but not much.

I think Ann Wood is right to say they are not a school because Teletubbies is made for children aged two to five and children of this age do not go to school yet so they should have the chance to enjoy television. Other programs like Play Days do try and educate children which is good but if they did this too much then the children would get bored with it and switch off. So its probobly best that childrens programmes do educate a bit and entertain a bit, then children will learn something and get entertained.

Teletubbies – Sample Essay 2

Anne Wood says, 'We are not a school, we are an entertainment programme for young children.' Do you think her view is right? Should children's television educate or entertain?

'At last, a children's programme that my toddler will watch', says a mother in the Letters Section of the Radio Times referring to the arrival of Teletubbies, a new programme for young children on the BBC.

I have not seen this programme but I've seen a lot of the publicity and 'hype' about it. Teletubbies has become very popular so clearly they are doing something right.

I can remember Playdays when it was Playbus and before this I used to enjoy Postman Pat, Rosie and Jim and even Sooty but this was when I was very little.

When your young I don't think you understand if a programme is educational or not, you watch it because you enjoy it. But I think it's true that if you enjoy something your more likely to watch it again and if it's educational then you will learn from what they are telling you. One programme that combines fun with learning is Sesamy Street which has been on television for years. I still enjoy watching this now and I think they put across things like the alphabet and counting in a fun but useful way. Although it's American I don't think this affects British children and it might be good for them to see children with differant accents and voices.

All children end up going to school so Anne Wood is right to say that Teletubbies isn't a school. I feel children should have the chance to watch something enjoyable as they will have plenty of time later for learning. It seems to me that the fuss is all about how the Teletubbies speak. I think this is exagerated because the whole programme can't be in Cantonese or 'burble incomprehensibly' or no-one would understand what was happening. As the Daily Mail article says, Bill and Ben and The Clangers also had 'flobbadob speech' and these programmes were not critisized for being a bad influence on children.

Perhaps the answer is for childrens programmes to be a mixture of entertainment and education. Theres probably nothing wrong with showing Teletubbies as long as children also see a more educational programme like Playdays or Sesamy Street. Children grow out of watching these progammes (I don't watch Sooty anymore) so as long as Teletubbies is not violent or a bad influence then it is ok for children to watch. It's unlikely to change as Anne Wood says, 'We have a responsibility to treat our audience with respect.'

Sample Essay – Teletubbies

Commentary

Anne Wood says, 'We are not a school, we are an entertainment programme for young children.' Do you think her view is right? Should children's television educate or entertain?

Sample Essay 1
Line:
1 Not a good technique just to echo the title
2 Note the mis-spelling of Anne
3 Some attempt at an introduction
4 An attempt to use an example from experience, even if it is limited. An attempt to show the popularity of the programme
8 Too much evidence in this area and a move away from the title
12 Bad organisation, the brother not cutting out pictures should have been mentioned after the sister
14 Some attempt at paragraphing for new points
15 Mis-use of this quotation, it was made by the programme's creators who were not complaining about the programme but stating the current situation
16 This point doesn't have a conclusion
18 Inaccurate point, they do not all speak in Cantonese
19 Confusing, it's not made clear who is speaking to them in English. We presume this means the parents. Another point that isn't developed
21 An attempt to use further evidence. The paragraph though has little to do with the question set.
23 This paragraph is the strongest as it starts to work on the title. Some evidence used from the article
25 This implies that when children go to school they stop enjoying television
27 Use of other evidence – Playdays. (Note the mis-spelling in the essay) and they recognise that it is an educational programme
29 A naïve view that children would get bored. Clearly from the letters, children do not get bored with Playdays
30 A recognition that children's programmes can educate and entertain.

Overall – A limited and probably unplanned argument. Very little use of evidence in the articles – some has been mis-used. No evidence drawn from other programmes they know. Technically very weak with mis-spellings of words used in the resource material. Repetitive phrasing, see paragraphs 2 and 3 and the conclusion.
The essay falls into the lower part of the third grading category, 18 – 13 D- to F+ (see page 96) and was awarded a grade of E.

Sample Essay 2
Line:
1 - 3 A good opening that uses a relevant quotation and gives the context. The student though doesn't follow it up other than the popularity point in line 5.

4 - 5 The student is honest although it does help to write about something you know about. Remember, students are often given a choice of questions. Appropriate use of the word 'hype' in inverted commas.

7 - 9 This paragraph links well with the last one and shows some sense of planning. The examples are useful and the Sooty one is referred to near the end.

10 - 13 A good point made about enjoyment and awareness, it could be phrased better but the idea is conveyed.

14 - 18 Sesame Street is an ideal example to choose in answering this question. The student recognises that the programme may be controversial being American. The point about accents is also thoughtful and could have been developed. Mis-spelling of Sesame is not a significant fault.

19 - 21 The student now moves to a fresh point which is valid but could have been expressed more succinctly.

22 - 26 A perceptive point concerning the speech problem. Unlike Essay 1, the student makes this relevant to the discussion and makes good use of the resource material. A useful quotation inserted although the grammar is incorrect.

27 - 28 Again, evidence of planning as the writer brings the points to a suitable conclusion – there is justification for both types of programme.

29 - 33 The student concludes with a new point rather than repeating an earlier one. The reference to Sooty again is excellent (the original suggested this was more chance than planning!) A well-chosen quotation is used and is the continuation of what Anne Wood said after the quotation in the title.

Overall – An essay that shows planning and perception although some points need developing. The essay has a few technical errors, more prominent near the end – a frequent fault. The student does well, particularly for someone who is not familiar with the programme. Expression is very good in places but a wider range and more confident use would give this essay top marks. The essay falls into the lower part of the top grade category 30 – 25, A* - B (see page 96) and deserves a B.

Woman with a winning punch – Sample Essay 3

Write the newspaper report of Jane Couch's next fight. You can decide the result of the fight, but your report should show whether or not the newspaper takes women's boxing seriously. Set out your report like a newspaper article.

Woman boxer dies in tragic fight

Yesterday evening at around 7 p.m. Jill Smith was pronounced dead after her title fight with the world champ Jane Couch. After a promising start in the first round for Jill, knocking down her formidable opponent, things started to go against her. She held up well in the second round resisting a flurry of punches from the 'Fleetwood Assassin' Jane Couch. After her first round knock-down she came into the second looking for payback. Jill came out on the attack but the power in Jane's punches wore her down, leaving her with her guard up until the bell. Round three started with a more cautious attitude from Jill, wary of being caught out again. Both boxers fought well through the uneventful third round, the calm before storm to take place in the next, and decisive round. It started much the same as round three with both fighters trading punches, then Jill Smith - age 32 went for the knockout.

Her confidence was boosted from her first round success and she was confident of the win. I spoke to her coach before the fight and this is what he had to say.

'She's a very talented boxer, she takes punches as well as she gives them. Her main chance of the win for her today is her left hook, it's so quick and powerful, Jane Couch hasn't got a chance.' The left hook the coach mentioned came into play in the fourth. After fighting quite defensively for most of the round, Jill suddenly launched a flurry of punches. Her left hook connected with Jane's chin, knocking her back onto the ropes. Jane covered up while Jill pounded her defences. A decisive punch that sent Jane to the canvas might have ended the contest at this moment, but the bell came in before the referee completed his count. The fifth round proved to be Jill's last, as in a twist of fate she slipped and stumbled. Jane seized the opportunity and hit Jill with such a force she was unconscious before she hit the canvas. The medics were called immediately and they took Jill to the medical facilities at the arena before moving her to hospital where she passed away the following day from being in a severe coma. Her family were too distressed to talk about the incident and Jane Couch declined an interview.

This tragic event casts a shadow over the future of women's boxing with the BBBC stating that their plans to licence women's boxing in this country have been scrapped. The Women's American Boxing Organisation have not made a formal announcement but they are rumoured to be following the BBBC's lead.

Sample Essay – Woman with a winning punch

Commentary

Write the newspaper report of Jane Couch's next fight. You can decide the result of the fight, but your report should show whether or not the newspaper takes women's boxing seriously. Set out your report like a newspaper article.

The layout should accurately conform to a newspaper layout:
- appropriate and dramatic headline starts the piece
- main issue of the story introduced in the first sentence
- the rest of the structure conforms to a newspaper report; a report of the fight and then conclusions and commentary from those concerned
- suitable additional quotations from Jill's coach.

The language used should contain significant elements of newspaper language and should be consistent either as tabloid or broadsheet:
- the language used is consistent with a middle-brow tabloid. Of the many examples there is, 'resisting a flurry of punches from the Fleetwood Assassin.' (Notice also the good use of the resource material to develop the piece).
- Other examples, 'The left hook the coach mentioned came into play in the fourth' 'Her family were too distressed to talk about the incident, and Jane Couch declined an interview.'

The attitude towards women's boxing should be consistent and clear, whether it is serious or frivolous and supports or is opposed to women's boxing:
- a serious attitude is maintained throughout the piece and the writer balances a dramatic report of the fight with the tragic conclusion.

Technically very good at the top end with few errors:
- the piece is not faultless but there are very few technical errors or inadequacies.
- competence is shown in the correct use and accurate spelling of such words as: pronounced, formidable, attitude, decisive, opportunity and immediately.

Other factors worthy of reward are:
- a well-organised piece, completed in the set time
- the piece is a good length. It is clearly paragraphed.
- the description of the incident is built up in a suitable dramatic style.
- the inclusion of the larger news story about the BBBC's involvement.

The student was awarded Grade A.